LEADING STUDENTS INTO PRAYER

Ideas and Suggestions from A to Z

MARY KATHLEEN GLAVICH, SND

TWENTY-THIRD PUBLICATIONS
Mystic, Connecticut 06355

ACKNOWLEDGMENTS

Scriptures are taken from the *New American Bible* copyright © 1986 by the Confraternity of Christian Doctrine, Washington, D.C. and are used with permission. All rights reserved.

"Prayer to the Guardian Angel" on page 58 from the English translation of *A Book of Prayers* © 1982 by the International Committee on English in the Liturgy (ICEL), Inc. All rights reserved.

The story on page 109 was adapted from *Taking Flight: A Book of Story Meditations* by Anthony de Mello, S.J., Doubleday, © 1988 and used with permission of the publisher.

The excerpt from *Our Treasured Heritage: Teaching Christian Meditation to Children* by Theresa O'Callaghan Scheihing with Louis M. Savary, © 1981 is reprinted by permission of The Crossroad Publishing Company.

The poem on page 8, the cheer on page 51, and the skit on pages 115-116 appeared in the *Christ Our Life* series written by the Sisters of Notre Dame and published by Loyola University Press.

"i thank You God for most this amazing day" is reprinted from ZAIPE by e.e. cummings, edited by George Firmage, by permission of Liveright Publishing Corporation. Copyright © 1950 by E.E. Cummings. Copyright © 1979, 1978, 1973 by Nancy T. Andrews. Copyright © 1979, 1973 by George James Firmage.

The prayer leaflet (Illustration T) first appeared in the *Gospel of Luke*, the *Little Rock Scripture Study for Children* written by Sr. M. Kathleen Glavich, S.N.D., and published by The Liturgical Press. It is reprinted here by permission of the Little Rock Scripture Office.

Special thanks to Sr. Mary Barbara Knuff, S.N.D., and her eighth graders at Notre Dame Elementary School for the prayers on pages 91, 92.

The author is also grateful to John van Bemmel and his associates at Twenty-Third Publications, all of whom contributed to the quality of this book, to Sr. Mary Agnes O'Malley, S.N.D., for graciously reading the manuscript, and to Sr. Mary Dolores Abood, S.N.D., for her generosity in proofreading the text.

Twenty-Third Publications
185 Willow Street
P.O. Box 180
Mystic CT 06355
(203) 536-2611
800-321-0411

ISBN 0-89622-549-6
Library of Congress Catalog Card Number 92-62204

DEDICATION

To J. Thomas McClain, S.J.,
who helped me to pray

Contents

Introduction   1

*A*tmosphere for Prayer   4

Creating the right atmosphere for prayer by having a special place for it, using religious objects like candles and incense, playing music, and preparing the students to enter into prayer.

*B*iblical Prayer   9

Ways to read the Bible, ready-made prayers in the Bible, praying the psalms, savoring the words, meditating on Scripture, understanding symbols, and memorizing verses.

*C*entering Prayer   19

Presenting centering prayer to students, how to do it.

*D*efinition of Prayer   22

The nature of prayer, what others think of prayer, samples of people's prayer.

*E*ucharist, the Greatest Prayer   27

Key concepts to teach, how to teach about the Eucharist, preparing to celebrate the Eucharist.

*F*amily Prayer   31

Involving parents in class prayer, suggestions for prayer in the home.

*G*immicks as Prayer Starters   33

Creative ways to prompt and aid prayer.

*H*ymns and Poems   37

Hymns and poems as prayers, using hymns and poems to teach about prayer.

*I*nspirational Pieces   41

Ways to use inspirational pieces in class, kinds of inspirational pieces that can help in teaching prayer.

*J*esus and Prayer   43

Jesus as model and teacher of prayer, the Lord's Prayer.

*K*inds of Prayer   45

Ways to present a variety of prayers, meditation, contemplation, spontaneous prayer, vocal prayer, informal prayer, communal prayer, spiritual reading, charismatic prayer, movement, one-liners, flag prayers.

*L*iturgical Prayer   53

Liturgy of the Hours, Christian prayer, paraliturgical services, sacraments, sacrament of penance.

*M*arian Prayer and Prayer to the Saints   56

Ways to honor Mary, prayer to Mary and the saints.

*N*oteworthy Prayers   60

Traditional prayers and how to teach them, the rosary, the Way of the Cross, devotions to the Blessed Sacrament, the Morning Offering, meal prayers.

*O*bservances   65

Celebrating seasons of the liturgical year (Advent, Christmas, Lent, Easter, and Pentecost), the Church Unity Octave, novena in honor of the Sacred Heart.

*P*urposes of Prayer   70

Prayers of petition, adoration, contrition, and thanksgiving; prayer requests and intentions.

*Q*ualities of a Good Pray-er   73

Availability, honesty, trust, and perseverance.

*R*esources for Prayer 76

Books for catechists, books for catechesis, audiotapes and records, videotapes, periodicals, posters, slides.

*S*ilence and Stillness 84

The importance of silence, teaching about silence and stillness.

*T*imes of Prayer 87

Choosing a time for prayer, special times for prayer, the sabbath.

*U*niverse, as a Springboard for Prayer 89

Prayer from nature, prayer from anything, prayer from experience.

*V*isuals to Prompt and Aid Prayer 95

Types of visuals, how to use visuals, making visuals.

*W*riting and Journaling 97

Keeping a journal, forms of writing prayers, a written meditation.

*X*perience of Prayer 101

Motivation for prayer, the practice of prayer, postures, relaxing exercises, developing the habit of prayer.

*Y*es, the Primary Attitude 106

Being open to God's will, how God answers prayer.

Z-z-z: Sleep and Other Obstacles to Prayer 108

Misconceptions of prayer, lack of time, distractions, discouragement, sleepiness.

Appendices 111

Introduction

One of the greatest gifts we can give our students is the gift of prayer. Prayer lends meaning and depth to life and transforms the pray-er into a person of hope, vitality, and serenity. Prayer accomplishes this transformation by its very nature, for it is nothing less than an encounter with God, the source of all life and goodness. Coming into contact with God strengthens our faith, energizes us to live as we are meant to, and deepens our love for God and others.

Prayer ought to be as natural as breathing. It is as essential. However, along with today's need for improved communication skills in general, there is a recognized need for skills in communicating with God. Witness the plethora of books and workshops on prayer and the interest in Eastern religions and gurus. When a Catholic publication made a survey on prayer, one woman responded, "It is not so much that I do not want to pray or can't pray. It is that I really do not know how to pray." People are hungering for guidance in deepening their spiritual life. They want to learn the art of prayer.

Youth today, perhaps more than ever before, need to be introduced to the power and delights of prayer. Too many young people blindly seek life's peak experiences in drugs, alcohol, and sex. Too many, disillusioned and floundering, are taking their own lives. By showing them how to pray, we show them a way to make life worthwhile. We lead them to a Father who loves them when they feel unloved, to a Savior who forgives them when they have failed, and to a Spirit who enlightens them when they are confused. We lead them to a Friend who cares when they are distressed and gladly shares their joys. We help them realize that there is Someone beyond us who is all-powerful, all-wise, all-just, and all-good, Someone who is in control, Someone who makes the universe make sense.

Teaching students how to pray helps them tap their inner resources, natural and supernatural, in order to live more fully. In the silence of their hearts and with the aid of God's grace, they become better persons and grow closer to their ultimate goal: total union with God.

Our students are at all stages in their prayer life. Perhaps some have never progressed beyond "God bless Mom, Dad, and everyone else." On the other hand, some students may be able to teach *us* about prayer. Teaching the variety of prayer forms developed over the centuries meets these individual differences. It enriches everyone's prayer life. Although a certain type of prayer might not appeal to all students, those who are not ready for it now might adopt it as their preferred way of praying some day in the future.

Leading Students into Prayer presents methods and activities to teach students of all ages about prayer and its many forms. Let us hope they discover that, as St. Thomas Aquinas said, in praying you can concentrate on words, or better, the sense of the words, or best of all, on the one to whom you are praying.

As teachers of prayer, we must realize that prayer is a delicate and personal subject. In the realm of prayer, we are treading on holy ground, mysterious ground. Remembering that God works in unique ways within each person, we must reverence the young pray-ers we journey with for a time. Tolstoy made this point effectively in his short story "The Three Hermits," a retelling of a Russian folk tale.

The Three Hermits

Once a bishop was traveling by boat. He noticed a group of people listening to a fisherman who was pointing to the sea. As the bishop drew near, everyone took off their caps and bowed. One said, "The fisherman was telling us about the hermits." "What hermits?" asked the bishop. "And what were you pointing at?" "Why, that little island over there," answered the fisherman. "That's where the hermits live. I met them when I was stranded on the island one night." The bishop peered across the water but couldn't see the island. "What are they like?" he asked.

"One is small and stooped with a long beard. He wears a priest's cassock and is very old. He is always smiling and his face is like an angel's. The second is taller and wears a tattered peasant coat. He too is very old with a broad beard. He is strong, but kindly and cheerful. The third has a beard that reaches to his knees. He is stern and wears only a piece of matting tied around his waist. They did everything in silence, communicating with each other by a glance."

The bishop sent for the captain and asked to be rowed ashore to meet the hermits. The captain said, "I've heard they are foolish fellows who understand nothing and never speak a word, any more than the fish of the sea." But when the bishop offered to pay him for the trouble, the captain agreed to go back to the island and send the bishop to it in a small boat.

When the bishop was taken to the island, he was met by the three hermits standing hand-in-hand on the shore. The bishop said to them, "I am called to keep and teach Christ's flock. I wanted to see you and to do what I can to teach you, also. Tell me, how do you pray?"

The oldest replied, "Three are ye, three are we, have mercy upon us." All three then chanted, "Three are ye, three are we, have mercy upon us." "Ah, you have heard something of the Trinity," said the bishop, "but you do not pray right. I will teach you the way God in Scripture tells us to pray." He taught them that God the Son had come to Earth to save us. He said, "This is how the Savior taught us to pray. Repeat after me, 'Our Father.'" The three repeated, "Our Father." The bishop said, "Who art in heaven." The second hermit couldn't say this line properly; and the oldest one, who had no teeth, mumbled indistinctly. The bishop stayed all day, teaching each line of the prayer, sometimes saying a word a hundred times. The middle hermit was the first to say the prayer alone. He repeated it until the others learned it.

When the moon appeared, the bishop rose to return to the ship. The hermits bowed low to him. As the bishop was rowed back to the ship, he could hear the voices of the hermits loudly repeating the Lord's Prayer.

Back on the ship, the bishop watched the island fade away. After dark, he sat at the stern thinking of the good old men and how pleased they were to learn the Lord's Prayer. He thanked God for sending him to teach them. Suddenly, across the sea he saw something white and shining coming closer and closer. "What is it?" he asked the helmsman. But as he said this, he realized that it was the three hermits. They were gliding upon the water all gleaming white and approaching the ship as quickly as though it were not moving. The steersman yelled in terror, "O Lord! They're running on the water as though it were dry land!"

The hermits overtook the boat and addressed the bishop, all three at once: "We have forgotten your teaching. When we stopped saying it, a word dropped out, and then another, and now it has all gone to pieces. Teach us again." The bishop leaned over the ship's side and said, "Your own prayer will reach the Lord. Pray for us sinners." And he bowed low before the old men. They turned and went back across the sea. All that night a bright light shone where they were lost to sight.

In the end, prayer is a highly personal matter between the individual and God. God is the one who is the director of our students' spiritual lives. All we can hope to be are good catalysts. As a friend of mine explains it, catechists are like matchmakers; we bring our students and God together and then bow out of the scene.

I believe that if we teach nothing else in religion class, we should teach prayer. Then God will teach the rest.

Finally, if we wish to lead the students into prayer, we must be familiar with the terrain. Meeting the Lord ourselves, frequently and in different ways, enables us to guide the students to God with confidence and with compelling enthusiasm and warmth. And of course, we must remember to pray for our students.

Atmosphere
for Prayer

Remove the sandals from your feet, for the place where you stand is holy ground.

Exodus 3:5

Prayer happens in crowded subways and in planes 30,000 feet above Earth, in noisy stadiums and in emergency rooms, at 2:00 a.m. and during the 5:00 p.m. rush hour. Good prayer can happen anywhere and any time. Some times and places, however, are more conducive to prayer than others. Being body-creatures with five senses, we are affected by our surroundings. We respond to the things of the world we live in and are conditioned by them. In reaching out for an experience of the sacred, the supernatural, we have found that certain actions and symbols speak to us of God and help lift our minds and hearts to the Lord. A striking example of this is the worship of Eastern Rite churches. Their gold, glory, and majesty fill us with a sense of God's awesome presence.

A first step in teaching prayer, then, is to teach the students those conditions and objects that pave the way for communing with God. Teach how to create a prayer atmosphere by providing it for them during classroom prayer experiences.

A Special Place
The Israelites considered places where God came and interacted with them as holy and special. Jacob marked the site of his dream with a memorial stone anointed with oil. Moses went to the meeting tent to commune with the Lord. The place where our students pray should be special, too.

• *Prayer house* • One teacher I know converted a five-foot reading hut from the Troll company into a prayer house for her first graders. She has it furnished with a crucifix, a children's Bible, and holy cards. The children enter one or two at a time for prayer. Cartons from large appliances (refrigerator) also make good prayer houses.

• *Church or chapel* • Take advantage of a parish church or chapel. Go there with your students for prayer services, quiet reflection, and personal visits.

• *Prayer corner* • Set up an attractive prayer corner in your classroom and encourage the students to make their own prayer corner at home. Near the prayer corner, post a picture related to the current topic in religion class. The following items may be arranged on or near a table to create a prayer corner:

the opened Bible on a stand
a colorful piece of material on the table
a banner hanging behind the table or before it
flowers or plants, real or artificial
a candle
a crucifix or a statue
a religious picture like an icon
a special chair, perhaps a rocking chair

• *Prayer room* • Process to a different room for class prayer to signify that something special is happening. You may have the luxury of a building with an extra room that can be converted into a prayer room. If so, provide large pillows or prayer kneelers, as well as the items suggested above for a prayer corner.

• *Your example* • Make sure the students see you praying sometimes in the church or chapel, in the prayer room, and at the classroom prayer corner, too.

Special Effects
• *Prayer mats* • Give the students carpet pieces or have them bring towels to use as prayer mats to sit on during times of prayer. You may prefer to have them make their own prayer mats. Here are two ways to make sit-upons:

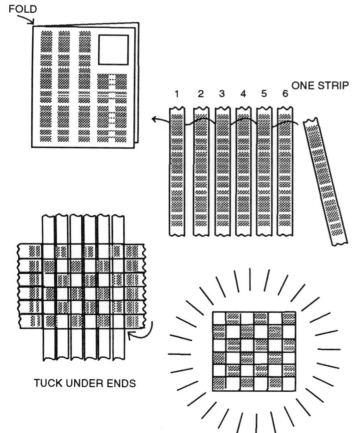

FOLD

1 2 3 4 5 6 ONE STRIP

TUCK UNDER ENDS

1. Distribute twelve double-page sheets of newspaper to each student and give these directions:

a. Take each folded sheet and, starting at the open edge, keep folding it over and creasing the folds to make uniform strips as wide as a column of print.

b. Place six strips in a vertical position. Weave the other six strips through them close together, making a tight weave.

c. Take the ends of the strips extending out around the mat and tuck them into the last row of weaving. No need for staples or tape.

d. Cover the mats with contact paper or vinyl so that they last longer and do not make black print marks on the students' clothes.

2. Give each child two rectangular pieces of wallpaper or plastic with holes punched about an inch apart around the edges. Have the students sew around three sides with yarn, ribbon, or cord, stuff the mat with newspaper or packaging material, and then sew up the last side.

• *Music* • Play soft music during prayer time, instrumental music or hymns that have the theme of the prayer period. Below are some classical pieces that facilitate prayer. Begin a collection of cassette tapes and records.

Composer and Selection	Mood
Bach, *Brandenburg Concerto #2*	ornate but gentle
Barber, *Adagio for Strings*	spiritual, awe
Bax, *The Garden of Fand*	fairy tale feeling
Beethoven, *Symphony #6* (Pastoral) side one	excellent for country scenes
Brahms, *Symphony #1*, 3rd movement	tranquil, graceful
Britten, *A Simple Symphony*, Op. 4	many short dramatic elements
Canteloube, *Songs of the Auvergne*	gentle, supportive
Los Chacos, *El Condor Pasa/La Flute Magique*	merry, exciting
Chopin, *Nocturne in E Flat Major*, Op. 9	poignant
Chopin, *Concerto in F Minor*, No. 2	strong, yet gentle
Copland, *Appalachian Spring*	wide variety of moods
Debussy, *Danse Sacrée et Danse Profane*	many moods
Debussy, "Sunken Cathedral"	robust, solemn
Delius, *In a Summer Garden*	a potpourri of emotions
Environments, "The Psychologically Ultimate Seashore"	natural sounds
Glazunov, *The Seasons*, Ballet, Op. 67	seasonal imagery
Grieg, *Peer Gynt Suites 1 and 2*	lilting, bouncy
Grofe, *Grand Canyon Suite*	sometimes serene, sometimes exhilarating
Holst, *The Planets*	warm, flowing
Liszt, *Liebestraum*	dreamy
Rachmaninoff, *Piano Concerto #2*	sometimes triumphant and martial, sometimes quiet, sentimental
Ravel, *Daphnis and Chloe*, Suite #2	excellent for beginning imagery
Respighi, *Pines of Rome, Fountains of Rome*	nature imagery
Rimsky-Korsakoff, *Scheherazade*	wide range of moods
Rodrigo, *Concierto de Aranjuez*, 2nd movement	gentle and pensive
Rossini, Overture to *La Gazza Ladra*	humor and irony

Sibelius, *The Swan of Tuonela*	sad and sentimental
Sinding, *Rustles of Spring*	bright and alive
Smetana, *Ma Vlast* ("The High Castle")	awesome structure
Smetana, *Moldau*	gentle, flowing
Tarrega, *Recuerdos de la Alhambra*	pensive, evocative
Tchaikovsky, *The Nutcracker Suite*, "Waltz of the Flowers"	delicate, graceful
Vaughan Williams, *Fantasia on Greensleeves*	warm, human relationships
Vivaldi, *The Four Seasons, Winter*	active release of feelings

• *Candles* • Light candles to set a mysterious, mystical tone to a prayer experience. Check local fire codes first. The lighting of the candles could be within a prayer service. Extinguish them at the end to bring closure to the activity.

• *Incense* • Burn incense, either grains or sticks. Protect the surface under the censer from sparks and ashes with plastic or some other safe material. Explain to the students that in Scripture prayers are compared to sweet-smelling incense that rises up to God.

• *Darkness* • Darken the room to create a prayerful atmosphere.

Setting the Mood
A transition is needed between ordinary class activities and prayer periods. There are various methods to provide this.

• *Recalling God's presence* • Before beginning prayer, let the students get settled and recall God's presence. You may merely recall Jesus' promise that where two or three are gathered in his name, he is in their midst.

• *Poems for quieting children* • Prepare young children for prayer by having them recite a poem like one of these:

> I have ten little fingers
> and they all belong to me.
> I can make them do things.
> Would you like to see?
> I can shut them up tight
> or open them wide.
> I can put them down
> or make them hide.
> Or hold them just so ...
> (*Fold hands.*)
>   Source Unknown

One, two:
　Here's what I do.
Three, four:
　To love Jesus more.
Five, six:
　On him my heart fix.
Seven, eight:
　Sit still and wait.
Nine, ten:
　Talk to my Friend,
Jesus.

• *Active preparation* • Before a prayer experience, little children may set up a prayer table while the class is listening to a song. One child covers the table with a cloth, another puts the candle on it, and another, the Bible.

• *Maintaining discipline* • Deal with discipline problems promptly. One day my twelfth graders were about to try a form of mental prayer. After I lit a candle to begin, Michael jumped out of his seat and blew it out. That was my cue to put Michael out of the room. If I hadn't, he would have spoiled the experience for the rest of the class.

• *Your example* • The students will take their cue from you. Convey peace and reverence by your words and actions, and your students will sense that prayer time is a special time.

See "X: Experience of Prayer," page 101.

Biblical Prayer

I ate it [the scroll], and it was as sweet as honey in my mouth.

Ezekiel 3:3

If prayer is communing with God, what better way is there to enter into it than through God's Word? The *Constitution on Divine Revelation* (21) states: "In the sacred books the Father who is in heaven comes lovingly to meet his children and talks with them." In the Bible, God speaks to us, revealing self as a loving God. Reading Scripture, then, is listening to God and thereby coming to know and love God. This is prayer. Moreover the Bible is a gold mine of ready-made prayers that we can adapt to our situations. In addition, we can use any verses as a launching pad to God by savoring the words and letting them penetrate our hearts.

When we introduce students to the treasures of the Bible, we give them the means to enrich their spiritual life abundantly. The activities that follow help students to be at home in the Bible, to appreciate it, and to use it for prayer.

Celebrating Scripture

• *Enthroning the Bible* • Hold a ceremony to enthrone the Bible to develop the sense of its sacredness in the students. Sing a song about God's Word, have a procession with the Bible and candles, and then place it on a pillow on a special table or shelf. Include a reading about Scripture such as verses from Psalm 119 or Matthew 7:24-27, the parable of the house built on rock. Let the students come up individually to kiss the Bible, bow to it, or lay their hand on it and pray, "Your word, O Lord, is a lamp for my feet."

• *Scriptural prayer services* • As a culminating activity for a unit or as a celebration of a feast or season or special time (like report card time), plan prayer services that include Scripture readings, time for reflection, and responses. Here is an outline:

Song
Introduction to the theme
Reading(s) from Scripture
Response: psalm
Quiet time
Prayer
Song

• *National Bible Week* • Observe National Bible Week, which is the Sunday before Thanksgiving to the Sunday after.

Reading the Bible
Teach your students various ways to read the Bible.

> **Bit-by-bit** Read only one or two lines and sink into them or let them sink into you. In this way you imitate Mary, the listening Virgin, who pondered God's ways in her heart.
>
> **Book-by-book** Read an entire book. Short books like the Gospel of Mark can be read in one sitting.
>
> **Bird's eye** Skim through a book, reading only the section headings, and then reflect on the impact of the whole.
>
> **One track** Using a concordance or other index, read according to a theme, such as prayer, faith, forgiveness, justice, women, or trees.
>
> **Methodical** Read the whole Bible straight through from beginning to end.
>
> **Liturgical** Read the readings for the day's eucharistic celebration.
>
> **Marian** Pray the rosary using mysteries from Scripture other than the traditional fifteen. Read a passage before each decade and then meditate on it during that decade.
>
> **Lucky Dip** Open the Bible at random and read.
>
> **Father David Knight's method** Keep the Bible on your pillow and every night read just one verse. You can always read one verse. Some nights you might read three or four. The number of pages covered is surprising. Before you know it, you will have read an entire book.

Using Ready-made Prayers
Pray ready-made prayers from the Bible before, during, and at the end of class.

• *Examples* • See the Book of Psalms, the prayer of Habakkuk (Habakkuk 3:17-19), Mary's Magnificat (Luke 1:46-55), and Paul's words, which are probably an early Christian hymn (Colossians 1:15-20).

• *One-line prayers* • Post one-line prayers from Scripture like the following and pray them in class:

> Speak, Lord, for your servant is listening. (1 Samuel 3:9)
> My spirit rejoices in God my savior. (Luke 1:47)
> Lord, I believe; help my unbelief! (Mark 9:24)
> My Lord and my God! (John 20:28)
> Come, Lord Jesus! (Revelation 22:20)

• *Visual reminders* • Have the students letter a short prayer from Scripture on a rock, a banner, a sheet of paper, a card, or anything else that they can display as a reminder to pray that prayer. A card with the verse can be used as a bookmark.

• *Scriptural songs* • Many popular Christian songs are scriptural passages set to music. Incorporate them into your lesson. The *Kids' Praise* series for young children and the *Psalms Alive* series are particularly good. Both are from Maranatha Music. See "R: Resources," page 76.

• *Mantras* • Teach your students to savor a word or a phrase from Scripture and to use it as a mantra. A mantra is a word repeated monotonously as a means to center oneself and come into the presence of God. The simplest biblical prayer is "Abba."

• *Scriptural prayer calendar* • Compile a calendar with a short prayer from the Bible for each day of the month. Each student may choose a page (date) to plan and decorate.

• *Scripture for the occasion* • Present different Scripture prayers and passages and ask the students when it would be particularly appropriate to pray them. Or give the students a list like the following and have them locate and read the corresponding references and tell why each would be good for its situation.

When I am troubled or confused	John 14:27
When I think of death	John 11:21-26
When I am in trouble	Matthew 11:28-30
When someone has hurt me	Matthew 18:21-35
When I have hurt someone	Matthew 5:23-24
When I am afraid or worried	Mark 4:35-41
When I want more than I have	Luke 21:1-4
When a friend has disappointed me	Luke 6:36-38
When I wonder if anyone loves me	John 19:28-30
When I am happy	Psalm 148
When I am thankful	Psalm 138; Luke 17:11-19
When I am frightened	Luke 12:32; John 14:1-4
When I need love	John 15:15; Philippians 1:7-9
When I am discouraged	John 16:22, 33; Matthew 6:28-34
When I am happy	Philippians 4:4-7; Psalm 23
When I need forgiveness	Matthew 9:6-13; Mark 11:24-25; Psalm 51
When I need healing	James 5:13-16; Mark 5:35-43
When I have deep sorrow	2 Corinthians 12:8-9; Philippians 2:13
When I feel hopeless	Mark 15:34; Psalm 13:1; Psalm 91:1, 5
When I am desperate	Psalm 69:1-3, 16; Philippians 4:13
When I face a challenge	Philippians 4:13; Isaiah 6:8; Exodus 3:11-12
When I am lonely	Mark 14:37; Acts 17:28; Matthew 28:20
When I fail	Mark 15:34; Ephesians 3:20-21; 2 Corinthians 12:7
When I am exhausted	Psalm 69:1, 4; 1 Corinthians 10:13; 2 Corinthians 12:7
When I am envious	1 John 2:15-17; Hebrews 13:14; 2 Corinthians 12:7-9

• *Slide meditation* • Have a group of students prepare a slide meditation with music to accompany scriptural passages that are centered on a theme such as faith, hope, or God's love.

• *Praying psalms* • Teach the students to pray the psalms in different ways:
1. Alternate sides in praying the verses.
2. Have a reader pray the entire psalm with all responding to each verse with an antiphon.
3. Pray the psalm together and then have individuals add to it by
   repeating a line that is particularly meaningful,
   paraphrasing a verse, or
   repeating a verse and adding to it.
For example, the praying of Psalm 23:1-4 might be as follows:

All:	The Lord is my shepherd; I shall not want.
	In verdant pastures he gives me repose;
	Beside restful waters he leads me;
	he refreshes my soul.
	He guides me in right paths
	for his name's sake.
	Even though I walk in the dark valley
	I fear no evil; for you are at my side
	With your rod and your staff
	that give me courage.
Student 1:	He refreshes my soul.
Student 2:	You are at my side.
Student 3:	He guides me in making right decisions.
Student 4:	I shall not want anything. I'll have all the peace and love I need.
Student 5:	I fear no evil, not even when people try to ruin my reputation.

• *Praying aloud* • Suggest to the students that they involve their bodies in praying Scripture by praying verses aloud. In this way their mouths say God's Word and their ears hear it.

Mining Scriptural Verses

• *The Sunday liturgy* • The main way that adult Catholics are in touch with Scripture is in the Sunday liturgies. Teach your students the practice of gleaning one significant verse from the Sunday liturgy to focus on during the week. They can post this verse, pray it, reflect on it, and use it in family prayers throughout the week.

• *Reading in class* • Offer the opportunity for quiet reading and praying over Scripture during class. Have your students go to church and spread out as far from one another as possible. Let them read passages turned to at random in their Bibles or provide them with study guides for a particular passage or theme.

• *Reflecting on a short selection* • Challenge the students to pray over just one line or a short verse of Scripture. Direct them to reflect on the literal meaning and its meaning for them, and then to speak to God about it. They might write their reflections and then share them.

• *Delving into a verse* • Have the students delve into each word or phrase in a scriptural verse, considering its everyday meaning, its meaning in the context of the passage, and its meaning in their life. After each reflection, they might compose a brief prayer flowing from the word. Present the following example:

"A lamp to my feet is your word" Psalm 119:105.

Lamp A lamp gives light and enables us to see. Because of lamps we can carry on our daily activities when it is dark. A flick of a switch floods a room with light. Lamps on the sides of roads guide traffic in the dark; lights guide airplanes and ships. God, thank you for the gift of light. Always be my light and let me be a light for others.

Feet Usually we don't pay attention to our feet. What a service they perform for us. They take us wherever we wish to go. God, guide my feet to good places. Let them hurry to be of assistance to others and to do good.

Word A word expresses our thoughts and feelings. It lets us know what others are thinking and feeling. Because of Jesus, the Word, and Sacred Scripture we are able to know and love God. Lord, let me read and study your word in the Bible and communicate it to others. Let me use it to guide my journey through life.

• *Personal verses* • Ask the students to reflect on the meaning a particular verse has for them and then to write a response to God. See Illustration A on pages 111-112 for a list of appropriate verses. Duplicate Illustration A and use one of the following means to distribute slips of paper with verses.

1. Put the verses in a box, perhaps a heart-shaped candy box. Pass around the box for each student to draw out a paper.

2. Insert the verses into balloons and then inflate the balloons. Or write the verses on inflated balloons, deflate the balloons, and then let each student take one to inflate and read.

3. Curl the slips of paper, using the edge of a scissor blade. Attach one end of each slip to the outline of a tree or heart or flowers so that the students can pluck the papers.

4. Put the verses in bugle snacks.

5. Substitute verses for the fortunes in purchased fortune cookies, using a safety pin and tweezers to remove the fortunes. Or make your own Scripture fortune cookies. Here is a recipe:

Scripture Fortune Cookies

3/4 cup butter
2 cups sugar
1 tsp. vanilla
3 eggs
1 cup sifted flour

Mix together butter and sugar. Add vanilla. Beat in eggs. Add flour. Drop by teaspoon on greased and floured cookie sheets, allowing 2 inches between. Bake 15 minutes at 375°. Promptly, while cookies are warm, set a folded verse on each and fold cookies in half.

• *A selection of verses* • Distribute a list of favorite biblical texts. Have the students choose one they like. Have them repeat it and relish it until they feel it's time to move to another one.

• *A word of salvation* • Tell the students that in the past Christians gave one another "a word of salvation." This was a scriptural verse that had special meaning for the recipient. Some people today include scriptural verses in letters. Give students a word of salvation that you have chosen for each of them personally. Encourage them to begin the practice of sending people meaningful scriptural verses, particularly at special times in their lives.

Personal Prayer That Flows from Scripture

• *Paraphrasing* • Invite the students to paraphrase prayers in the Bible. The psalms lend themselves to this activity. Try one yourself and share it with your students. Psalm 23 works well. Have the students rewrite Psalm 23 based on an image of God other than a good shepherd. Alfredo chose to compare God to a counselor. He ended with, "Best of all, God's services are free!"

• *Acrostic prayers* • Some psalms are alphabetic; each verse begins with a letter of the Hebrew alphabet. Have your students write prayer acrostics using the letters in their names. For instance, Erin wrote:

E njoy the Lord!
R ejoice in his name.
I n the Lord is our salvation.
N ever forget who he is.

For an *E* in her name, Maureen wrote, "Eternal rest grant unto you, O Lord"!

• *Putting students' names in verses* • Personalize passages of the Bible by inserting or substituting your students' names. Ephesians 1:3-14 is good for this. Here is the beginning of it with names substituted for first and second person pronouns.

Blessed be the God and Father of our Lord Jesus Christ, who has blessed Margaret in Christ with every spiritual blessing in the heavens, as he chose Tony in him, before the foundation of the world, to be holy and without blemish before him. In love he destined Barbara for adoption to himself through Jesus Christ, in accord with the favor of his will, for the praise of the glory of his grace that he granted Mary in the beloved.

In him, Carol has redemption by his blood, the forgiveness of transgressions, in accord with the riches of his grace that he lavished upon Michael. In all wisdom and insight, he has made known to Rosa the mystery of his will in accord with his favor that he set forth in him as a plan for the fullness of times, to sum up all things in Christ, in heaven and on earth.

Teach the students to read Scripture passages inserting their own name, as:

If, Kathleen, you want to be a follower of mine, renounce yourself, take up your cross every day, Kathleen, and follow me. What good is it, Kathleen, for you to have won the whole world and to have lost or ruined your very self? (Luke 9:23-25)

• *A motto* • Challenge students to find a verse to adopt as a motto.

• *Creative prayers* • Be creative in using Scripture for prayer. One of our high schools was chosen a National School of Excellence. At the public celebration the principal led everyone in a closing litany based on the story of creation. She made statements expressing the work and the contribution of people that had made the award possible. After each statement, the auditorium full of people responded "That's good!" For instance, "Forty-two dedicated teachers come to school each day.... That's good!" The total effect was delightful and very moving.

Meditating on Scripture

Teach students how to meditate on a scriptural story by guiding them through one. You might be surprised how well your students respond to this type of meditation. Here is a method that is simple and effective.

Still the body. Have the students still their mouths, hands, and feet. Ask older students to refrain from jiggling their feet nervously. Tell younger ones to have listening hands and feet. Have them close their eyes. Adolescents will feel freer if you stand in the back of the room. Enter into the meditation with the class, but don't close *your* eyes.

Quiet the mind. Tell them to focus on God, present here, loving them, waiting to speak to them.

Read the scriptural passage.

Recreate the story in the imagination. Guide them through it again, suggesting insights, description.

Reflect on the story. Make it personal. Be a facilitator. Ask questions.

Respond to Scripture. Lead the students to respond in the form of a prayer or resolution—or both. Suggest topics of conversation.

See Illustration B, page 113, for a sample meditation.

These scriptural stories are good for meditation:

The boy Jesus in the Temple (Luke 2:41-50)
Temptation in the desert (Matthew 4:1-11)
Calling the first disciples (Luke 5:1-11)
Calming the storm (Luke 8:22-25)
Healing of a leper (Luke 5:12-16)
Healing of a paralyzed man (Luke 5:17-26)
Jesus and the sinful woman (Luke 7:36-50)
Blessing the children (Luke 18:15-17)
Healing a blind beggar (Luke 18:35-43)
Miracle of the loaves (John 6:1-13)
Jesus and Zacchaeus (Luke 19:1-10)
The widow's offering (Luke 21:1-4)
The rich young man (Matthew 19:16-22)
The raising of Lazarus (John 11:1-44)
Driving out the money-changers (Mark 11:15-17)
The Last Supper (Luke 22:14-23)
Washing the disciples' feet (John 13:1-11)
Agony in the garden (Luke 22:39-46)
The crucifixion (Luke 23:33-49)
On the way to Emmaus (Luke 24:13-35)

• *Making a scriptural symbol* • Here is an engaging way to lead the students to meditate on Scripture. Give a piece of aluminum foil to each student and explain that the class will experience a prayer-in-action. Ask the students to decide what their favorite Gospel story is: a miracle, a teaching of Jesus? Tell them to think of a symbol to represent this story. Direct them to make this symbol out of the aluminum foil, silently and prayerfully, thinking about what the story means to them and speaking to Jesus about it. After about three minutes, invite the students to turn to someone nearby and explain their symbols to each other. You can use clay the same way. I've heard it called "pray-dough." Pipe cleaners also work.

• *Written reflections* • Teach the students to make written reflections on Gospel passages. They will learn about themselves and their relationship with God.

• *Understanding biblical symbols* • Help your students to become knowledgeable about symbols used in the Bible, for instance, water. We pray in Psalm 42:2-3: "As the hind longs for the running waters, so my soul longs for you, O God. Athirst is my soul for God, the living God." How much more meaning these words have when we are aware of the significance of water in the Bible. The Israelites were nomads who traveled through the desert; water was precious to them.

The symbol of water is found in the Bible from beginning to end. In Genesis the garden of Eden is watered by a river that splits into four rivers. In Exodus, when the Israelites are wandering in the desert at God's direction, Moses strikes a rock and water gushes forth. In the Gospel of John, Jesus exclaims, "Let anyone who thirsts come to me and drink" (John 7:37). In the Book of Revelation where the new heaven and new earth are described, the one who sat on the throne says, "To the thirsty I will give a gift from the spring of life-giving water" (Revelation 21:6). An angel shows the writer a river sparkling like crystal, flowing from the throne of God and of the Lamb. On either side of the river grew the tree of life.

Then there is the water of Baptism. As Jesus tells Nicodemus: "No one can enter the kingdom of God without being born of water and Spirit" (John 3:5). Water plays a role in the wedding of Cana and in Jesus' meeting with the Samaritan woman. All of these references to water in the Bible can come into play and enrich our praying of Psalm 42, if we are aware of them.

We can trace and ponder the appearances of many other symbols in Scripture like rock, birds, bread, fire, and trees. The more we teach our students the Bible, the more they will perceive the nuances of the words and the more depth their prayer will have.

Memorizing Verses

Encourage students to memorize key verses that will come to mind when they need them. Janaan Manternach calls this "banking prayers." One Christmas evening my sister called with the news that my father had had a heart attack and had been anointed. I went to the hospital that night and then returned home. Throughout the night the words of Psalm 23 kept running through my mind: "The Lord is my shepherd." The next morning when I returned to the hospital I was introduced to the nurse who had worked overtime on Christmas day to stay with Dad all through the night. The nurse's name was Bob Shepherd.

• *Making a verse your own* • Help the students memorize not by rote, but by heart. Help them make the scriptural words their own. Discuss the meaning of the words and give your students time to think about them and to share what they mean.

• *Posted verses* • Suggest that the students post a verse of the week on a refrigerator or mirror.

• *Games for memorizing* • Use the following games and activities to help the students memorize verses in class and at home.

1. Write a verse on the board. Erase a word at a time. After you erase a word, have the class repeat the verse. Continue until all words are erased and the class is saying the verse by heart.

2. Write verses on strips of paper and cut them in half. Distribute them and tell the students to find the half that matches theirs and then memorize the verse.

3. Have the students each letter a verse on tagboard, cut it into puzzle pieces, and put the pieces into an envelope. Let them trade envelopes, put the puzzles together, and memorize the verses.

4. Let the students throw a ball, beanbag, or stuffed animal to one another. Each student who receives the item must recite a chosen verse or a word from a verse.

5. Letter, or have the students letter, verses on index cards. Keep the cards in a box or special pocket for the students to study.

6. On the board or on a transparency present verses that have blanks for key words. Have the class supply the missing words.

7. Hold races. Use charts, stickers, and stars to encourage memorizing verses.

Centering
Prayer

I am in my Father and you are in me and I in you. John 14:20

Grandma and Grandpa sit for hours on the porch, watching the leaves fall, the squirrels play, and the sun set. No words are necessary. The two bask in the sure, steady flow of their love for each other.

Three-year-old Julie crawls onto her dad's lap while he is watching football. As he holds her, she falls asleep. Their love is expressed and strengthened by their presence to each other.

This same nonverbal love that human beings experience with each other is the core of the prayer of the heart or centering prayer. Centering prayer is founded on the belief that God dwells within us. John of the Cross said: "O thou soul, most beautiful of creatures who longest to know where the beloved is, thou art thyself that very tabernacle where he dwells." Centering prayer is basically loving attention to God dwelling within us. It has its roots in the prayer tradition of the church fathers and desert fathers and incorporates the prayer techniques of the Eastern church.

Some students may already be practicing this simple form of prayer but not identifying it as centering prayer. Others might be drawn to centering prayer if they knew about it. After several days of doing centering prayer in religion class, one seventh-grade teacher had her students write evaluations Out of thirty-five responses, only two were negative. Seventh graders!

Introducing Centering Prayer
• *Explanation* • To prepare the students for centering prayer, write the words *person*, *place*, and *thing* on the board. Tell the students that although God is everywhere, we are sometimes most conscious of God in a certain person, place, or thing. We sense God's presence there in a special way. Ask the students to recall a time when they felt very close to God. Let them share their experiences. Then ask, "Have you ever sensed God's presence in yourself?" Point out that we know from Scripture that God is within us (John 14:20, for example). Explain to the students that it seems logical that the easiest way to get in touch with God would be to find God in ourselves. In centering prayer we do just that.

• *A story* • Tell this story or a similar story: Long ago in France St. John Vianney, the Curé of Ars, noticed that an old man spent hours in the parish church. The peasant would sit motionless, doing nothing. Finally one day the priest asked him, "What are you doing when you sit here?" The man replied, "I look at him and he looks at me." In centering prayer we look at God and block out everything else from our minds.

Explaining Centering Prayer

• *A skit* • Use the skit in Illustration C, pages 115-116, that explains how to do centering prayer. Call on volunteers to take the five parts in the play. Have them read from the front of the room. Instruct the class to listen for aspects of the prayer that appeal to them. When the play is finished, ask the students what they like about this prayer.

• *List of steps* • On the board list the five steps of centering prayer and explain them:

1. **Quiet down.** Sit upright so your head is well supported by your spine. Keep your eyes gently closed so energy is not wasted seeing. To relax, breathe slowly three times: exhale, take in fresh air, hold it, exhale.
2. **Move toward God within you.** Think only of God who is living deep within you and ponder God's love for you. Be present to God. Let the overwhelming love and goodness attract you. Rest in God's presence.
3. **Respond with a word (phrase).** Some suggestions: "I love you," "My Lord and my God," "Jesus." Repeat the prayer word slowly in your mind.
4. **Attend to God and enjoy God's presence.** When you know you are aware of things other than God, use your prayer word to bring you back. Don't stop to think about how you're doing. Focus on giving God your loving attention.
5. **Pray a prayer.** Use the Our Father or another prayer to make the transition out of centering prayer.

Experiencing Centering Prayer

• *Directions* • Guide the children into the prayer of the heart with these directions: Sit straight and still. Close your eyes and think only of God dwelling deep within you. Think of God's great love for you. Pray with me: "Jesus, I believe that you are present in the center of my being, loving me. In these next few minutes I want to remember that I am all yours. Let me come into your presence. Draw me to yourself, Jesus." Remain still. Repeat your prayer word in your mind. Stay with Jesus who loves you.

• *Follow-up* • After a centering prayer experience, ask the students to write their responses to it. Did they like it? What did they feel like? Could they sense God's presence? Then let some students respond orally if they choose to. Ask how many would like to use part of the religion class again for centering prayer.

Motivating Students to Practice Centering Prayer

• *Planning* • Explain to students that if they practice centering prayer every day, even for only five minutes, they will appreciate it more and more and miss it when they skip it. Have them decide on a time and place for personal centering prayer.

• *Making prayer cards* • Have the students make prayer cards, using their prayer word, as a reminder to practice centering prayer. Distribute index cards and have the students fold them so that they stand. Have them choose a prayer word and with pencil design it in large letters on the front of the card. Instruct them to color in the letters heavily with crayons and then paint over the entire surface of the card with black or blue tempera. The paint will adhere to the background completely but leave only streaks on the letters. Encourage the students to keep their cards in an easy-to-see place in their rooms at home.

Definition
of Prayer

To you I pray, O LORD. Psalm 5:3

There's a story of a sea captain who was caught in a terrific storm. He had weathered many a storm before, but this one was unusual. After trying everything to save the ship, as a last resort, the sea captain fell to his knees and prayed, "O God, I haven't bothered you for the last twenty years. Save me and I won't bother you for another twenty." Obviously the sea captain did not understand prayer. Neither did the little girl who wrote to God, "Dear God, Sometimes I think of you even when I'm not praying."

In teaching students to pray, start at square one by leading them to consider what prayer is. Prayer might be a natural habit for them, like eating. We eat three times a day, and we've eaten all our lives. However, a study of the digestive system in biology and nutrition in home economics makes us more inclined to be better eaters. Similarly, focusing on what prayer is improves one's prayer life.

Here are some activities that lead students to reflect on the nature of prayer and help them integrate prayer into their lives.

• *Completing sentences* • Draw on the students' knowledge of prayer. Have them complete the sentences:

Prayer is _____

I pray when _____

I pray because _____

Discuss the answers as a class or in small groups. Compile the list at the board or duplicate it for all the students.

• *Wonder and prayer* • Ask the students to recall a time when they were caught up in wonder at something. Invite them to share it with the class, describing what they saw and experienced and how they felt. Point out that they were probably launched into prayer whether they knew it or not.

• *Quotations about prayer* • Discuss or post statements about prayer like these:

"Let us leave the surface and, without leaving the world, plunge into God." (Pierre Teilhard de Chardin)

"God sits on top of our heart. When we desire to pray, the heart cracks open and God tumbles down inside." (A Hasidic explanation of prayer)

"Prayer oneth the soul to God." (Julian of Norwich)

• *Reflecting on definitions* • Present various definitions of prayer. Discuss them, asking:

Which one is best? Why?
Which one do you like most?
Which do you agree with? Disagree with?

Definitions of prayer
Prayer is the lifting up of the mind and heart to God.
Prayer is talking to God.
Prayer is putting your hand in God's hand.
Prayer is resting in the Lord.
Prayer is enjoying the company of a Friend.
Prayer is the most important communication we ever have.
Prayer is reciting words to an invisible Person.
Prayer is a last resort.
Prayer is wasting time gracefully.
Prayer is joy that mounts up to God in thanksgiving. (Isaac the Syrian)
Prayer is a conversation with one whom you know loves you. (St. Teresa of Avila)
Prayer is our humble answer to the inconceivable surprise of living.
(Rabbi Abraham Heschel)

• *Original definitions* • Have the students write their own definitions of prayer. Discuss prayer in class and then have the students revise their definitions.

• *A class definition* • Through discussion arrive at a class definition of prayer that is acceptable to all.

• *God's direct line* • Comment that God has an 800 number and also answers to 911. When you call God, you never get a busy signal, you are never put on hold, and you never hear an answering machine say, "This is God. I'm not in my office now..." Have the students write a conversation they might have with God if they phoned heaven.

• *A love relationship* • Compare prayer to communication in a love relationship. At first the two persons talk a lot. Then they are comfortable in just being silent together. As the relationship develops, they are able to communicate with a glance and eventually to read each other's minds. They can sit for hours enjoying the pleasure of each other's company. In a real love relationship, neither person is concerned about getting something out of it. These same characteristics describe the deepening of our relationship with God.

• *Comic strips* • Collect comic strips related to prayer. You'll be surprised how many you can find. Mount them on tagboard and laminate them or cover them with clear contact paper. Before an introductory class on prayer, distribute the cards and ask the students to analyze them for what they teach about prayer: when to pray, why to pray, how to pray, or attitudes toward prayer.

• *Developing a lesson with comic strips* • Use comic strips mounted on cards as an integral part of a development lesson on prayer. Mark each card with a different letter of the alphabet and write its letter in your lesson plan where it best fits. Distribute the cards to volunteers to read aloud when you call their letter. Then during your lesson on prayer, whenever a particular comic applies, call its letter and have the student who has that card read the comic strip. For instance, as you teach the purposes of prayer, one student might read the Family Circus cartoon that shows a boy in pajamas saying, "I'm gonna say my prayers, Daddy. Is there anything you want?"

• *People in Scripture who prayed* • Acquaint your students with famous scriptural stories of people who prayed:

    Abraham bargaining with God to spare a city (Genesis 18:20-32)
    Moses as he extends his arms in prayer during a battle (Exodus 17:8-13)
    Hannah longing for a son (1 Samuel 1:9-20)
    Judith before she ventures into the enemy camp (Judith 9:1-14)
    Esther before she risks her life to save her people (Esther 4C:12-30)
    Job when he endures much suffering (Job 40:4-5)
    Jesus in the Garden of Olives (Mark 14:35-36)
    Paul writing to the Philippians (Philippians 1:9-11)

• *Spiritual growth* • Discuss spiritual growth and how prayer contributes to it.

• *Sentence completion* • Ask the students to complete this sentence with the name of an object and an explanation: Prayer is like (a) _____ because _____. Sample: Prayer is like a paper clip because it holds the pages of my life together.

• *Prayer from other faith traditions* • Read prayers from other faith traditions. Discuss what they have in common. Here are four prayers you might use:

Jewish Prayer
Were our mouth filled with song as the sea is with water,
    and our tongue with ringing praise as the roaring waves;
were our lips full of adoration as the wide expanse of heaven,
    and our eyes sparkling like the sun or the moon;
were our hands spread out in prayer as the eagles of the sky
    and our feet as swift as the deer …
we should still be unable to thank thee and to bless thy name.
    From "The Sabbath Liturgy," *The Daily Prayer Book*

Hindu Prayer
From the unreal lead me to the Real!
From darkness lead me to the light!
From death lead me to immortality!
Om.

Hymn of African Pygmy Tribes
In the beginning was God.
    Today is God.
    Tomorrow will be God.
Who can make an image of God?
He has no body.
He is as a word
        which comes out of your mouth.
That word! It is no more.
        It is past, and still it lives!
So is God.

Native American Prayer
O great Spirit,
I need your strength and wisdom.
Let me walk in beauty
and make my eyes ever behold the red and purple sunset.
Make my hands respect the things you have made
and my ears sharp to hear your voice.
Make me wise so that I may understand
the things you have taught my people.
Let me learn the lessons
you have hidden in every leaf and rock.
Make me always ready to come to you
with clean hands and straight eyes.
So when life fades, as the fading sunset,
my spirit may come to you without shame.

• *Personal experiences* • Share your personal experiences with prayer, your successes and your failures.

• *Witness talks* • Invite a parishioner or several parishioners to give witness talks about prayer in their lives. Sponsor a talk by a well-known person. As I write this, St. Ignatius High School is preparing for a talk tonight by Lenny Wilkens, coach of the Cavaliers, the Cleveland basketball team. The title is "The Importance of Prayer in a Busy Person's Daily Life."

• *Interviews* • Have the students interview people they know, asking them how they pray, what their favorite prayers are, when they pray. Let the students share the results of these interviews in small groups.

• *An essay* • Have the students write an essay "What Prayer Means to Me" as a way of getting in touch with their convictions and experiences.

• *A collage* • Guide the students in making a collage on prayer, incorporating words related to prayer and appropriate pictures.

• *A dictionary* • Have the students make a dictionary of prayer in which they include terms related to prayer and the names of prayer.

• *A poster or bulletin board* • Direct the students to make a poster or bulletin board on prayer or do so yourself. Possible captions:

"A life hemmed with prayer is less likely to unravel."
"Seven days without prayer makes one weak."
"Life is fragile. Handle with prayer."
"Let your knees take some of the strain off your heart."
"You and God are the majority."
"Courage is fear that has said its prayers."
"Prayer changes people and people change the times."

• *Audiovisuals* • Use audiovisual programs on prayer after reading the teacher guides, which may be very helpful. See "R: Resources," page 76.

• *Literature on prayer* • Read a poem or passage from literature as a springboard for a discussion on prayer:
More things are wrought by prayer than this world dreams of.
Ulysses, Alfred Lord Tennyson

He prayeth best who loveth best
All creatures great and small.
The Rime of the Ancient Mariner, Samuel Taylor Coleridge

• *Prayer stories* • Tell a story in which people prayed. You might find such a story in a periodical like *Catholic Digest* and *Guideposts*, in your diocesan paper, or even in the daily newspaper.

• *Promoting prayer in the parish* • Have the students produce an insert for the parish bulletin encouraging people to pray.

Eucharist
the Greatest Prayer

"Do this in memory of me." Luke 22:19

We have always known that the Eucharist is central to our faith. As the dwindling number of priests threatens our celebrations of the sacred mysteries, we are coming to recognize even more the role of the Mass in our lives. It is crucial to pass on to our children the importance and value of the Eucharist.

Key concepts of the Eucharist to teach

The Mass is our highest form of worship in which we praise and thank God.

The death and resurrection of Jesus are made present during Mass carrying out our salvation.

As Jesus offers his sacrifice at Mass, we are able to offer him and also offer ourselves.

The Mass has two main parts in which God nourishes us: the Liturgy of the Word and the Liturgy of the Eucharist.

Jesus is present at the celebration of the Eucharist in the priest, the gathered assembly, the Word, and the sacred bread and wine.

Jesus is truly present in the sacred bread and wine. When we receive the host and cup, we receive him, body and blood.

The Eucharist expresses and brings about the unity and life of the church.

When we gather as a community to celebrate, each member is responsible for participating actively.

Teaching an Understanding of the Mass and Its Parts

• *Recalling experiences* • Let your students talk about special Masses in which they have participated.

• *Interviews* • Have your students interview three people about the Mass, asking what it means to them and why they participate.

• *An outline of the Mass* • To teach the order of the Mass, provide each student with an outline to fill in as you develop each part. Use missalettes if possible. See Illustration D, page 117, for a sample.

• *Forms of prayer in the Mass* • Have your students go through the Mass in a missalette and find prayers of adoration, contrition, thanksgiving, and petition. List them on the board under the respective headings.

• *Flashcards* • Distribute flashcards for the parts of the Mass. Have the students arrange them correctly in a pocket chart or hold them in the correct order in front of the class. You may wish to make the parts of each section of the Mass on different colored tagboard. You might give each student a set of flashcards to put in order.

• *Role models* • Pair younger students with older students for school Masses so that the older children can serve as models.

• *Songs for the Eucharist* • Choose an opening song, a presentation song, a communion song, and a closing song that express key concepts of the Eucharist. Have your students analyze the words of these songs to learn about the Mass.

• *Vessels and vestments* • Take your class to church and show and explain the vessels and vestments used for Mass, or invite a priest to do this. Have the students make a booklet about these objects or give them a prepared booklet to complete as they tour the church.

• *Eucharistic prayers* • Have the students compare the four main eucharistic prayers. Enact a eucharistic prayer in class, using a sacramentary.

• *Seder meal* • Celebrate a Jewish seder meal with your class to teach the roots of our Eucharist. See *Leading Students into Scripture,* Illustration O, pages 89-91, for the ritual.

• *A bulletin board* • Design, or let the students design, a bulletin board illustrating that Eucharist is thanksgiving.

• *Votive Masses* • Make your students aware of the many votive Masses. Show a list of titles on an overhead transparency or read them from a sacramentary.

• *Masses of different cultures* • Plan for your students to participate in Masses as celebrated by people of different cultures: Hispanic, Native American, African-American, Byzantine, Maronite. You might give them a taste of Latin, too.

Preparing Students for Celebrating Eucharist
• *Doing a reading at Mass* • Prepare readers to proclaim the Word at Mass by teaching them to enunciate, use expression, and project their voices. Let them practice in front of class, with a tape recorder, or at the church lectern.

• *Planning a Mass* • Guide your class in planning a Mass as a culmination of their study. Small groups may each prepare a part of the Mass (songs, readings, intercessions, Communion reflection), or the class may work as a whole. See Illustration E, page 118, for a planning chart.

• *Guest speakers* • Invite parishioners to speak about their roles in the Mass—a priest, deacon, server, lector, eucharistic minister, choir director, musician, usher.

• *Mass responses* • Practice the Mass responses with your students. Write the priest's prayers on slips of paper and put them in a box. Then call students to draw a slip and read it for the class to respond.

• *Gestures and postures* • Discuss the gestures and postures of the priest and the congregation during Mass.

• *Mass etiquette* • Have the class draw up rules for etiquette during the Mass.

• *Student homilies* • Challenge your students to write their own homily based on the readings for a particular Sunday Mass.

• *Communion prayers* • Have your students write original Communion prayers.

• *Thanksgiving after Communion* • Teach your students to use the word *altar* as a reminder of what to say to Jesus after receiving him in Communion:
    a = adore
    l = love
    t = thank
    a = ask
    r = resolve

• *Bringing a friend* • Encourage your students to invite a friend to Mass with them.

• *A liturgy team* • To enliven school liturgies, organize a liturgy team to plan Masses that involve the whole school. For instance, each class can contribute to a banner that will be displayed during the eucharistic celebration.

Reinforcing Concepts Related to the Mass
• *A guidebook* • Help your class make a book on the Mass. Older students may make a large book for younger children, perhaps the First Communion class.

• *Riddles* • Compose, or have your students compose, riddles on the parts of the Mass. Example: I am the prayer that summarizes what we believe. You pray me after the homily. What am I? (The Creed)

• *Word search* • See Illustration F, page 119, for a word search on Mass terms.

• *Word scramble* • Scramble words related to the Mass and have the students unscramble them and use each word in a sentence.

• *Fill in the blanks* • Pray the Mass prayers like the Glory to God and the Creed, omitting words for the students to supply.

• *Posters* • Have your students work in groups to design posters about the Eucharist. Post these in your parish hall.

• *Clay cup and host* • Help your students make cups and hosts out of clay. Here is a recipe for sparkling white clay:

Sparkling White Clay

1/2 cup corn starch
1 cup salt
3/4 cup water

Mix together in cooking pot. Set over low heat. Stir until the consistency of clay. Remove from pan and allow to cool slightly on aluminum foil. Shape into ball and place in plastic container. If clay starts to harden, add a small amount of water.

• *Last Supper mural* • Guide your students in making a mural of the Last Supper. Give young children patterns of human figures to trace, color, and cut out.

• *Picture of bread and wine* • Have your students make a striking arrangement of a cup and bread, wheat and grapes on paper. They might draw and color each element separately and then cut them out and arrange them on a blank sheet of paper. Give younger children patterns to trace.

Family Prayer

Hear, O Israel! The LORD is our God, the LORD alone! Therefore, you shall love the LORD, your God, with all your heart, and with all your soul, and with all your strength. Take to heart these words which I enjoin on you today. Drill them into your children. Speak of them at home and abroad, whether you are busy or at rest.

Deuteronomy 6:4-7

Father Patrick Peyton's saying, "The family that prays together stays together," is an important message for today's world. Do what you can to encourage family prayer. The parents are the primary educators of their children, and the habits and values assumed in the home can last a lifetime.

• *Family participation* • Invite the families of your students to the prayer celebrations and eucharistic celebrations of your class or school.

• *Memorizing prayers* • Elicit parental help in teaching your students to memorize their prayers.

• *Take-home sheet* • Send a sheet home to the parents of your students suggesting different ways the family can pray together. Here are some ideas to include:

Prayer in the Family

Pray meal prayers together. Hold hands as a sign of unity. At the end of a meal, exchange a sign of peace.

Set aside time each week for family prayer. This period can include reading the Bible.

Bless your children before they go to bed at night. Trace the Sign of the Cross on their foreheads and say, "God bless you."

Bless your children after a special meal.

Pray as a family before long trips, before major decisions, or when a family member, relative, or friend is sick.

Pray with your children at special moments. For instance, while witnessing a spectacular sunset, recall the greatness of God and pray a prayer of thanks and praise.

Take advantage of the opportunities you have each day for a religious discussion with your children.

Prepare for Sunday liturgies at a special family meeting beforehand. Glean an idea from one of the readings as a thought for the week. Post it on the refrigerator. Decide on something you wish to give thanks for as a family during the week's Eucharist.

Meditate with your children before they go to bed.

Observe the Lord's day by making Sunday a family day. At a family meeting, brainstorm for ideas of things your family could do together to make Sunday special. (Going out to breakfast, visiting a relative or friend, having a special meal, inviting someone to visit, going for a ride) Write these down and check them off when you do them. You might adopt one or two as a family tradition.

Compose a prayer together that you can pray as a family on Sundays.

Celebrate the liturgical seasons and feasts with your children.
(Include ideas here for celebrating Advent, Christmas, Lent, and Easter from Chapter 15, "O: Observances," page 65.)

Receive the sacrament of reconciliation as a family. Pray together and examine your consciences at home ahead of time. While each family member is in the reconciliation room or confessional, the other members can be praying for that person. Afterwards celebrate your experience of forgiveness with ice cream or pizza.

• *Parent meeting* • Hold a parent meeting for the purpose of encouraging family prayer. Let the program include time for parents to share ways their family prays together. Distribute and discuss a handout with suggestions as in the previous point.

• *Family book of prayers* • Alert the parents of your students to the book *Catholic Household Blessings and Prayers*, published by the U.S. Bishops' Committee on the Liturgy (Office of Publishing and Promotion Services, U.S. Catholic Conference, 3211 Fourth St., N.W., Washington, D.C. 20017, $18.95). This book contains prayers for every day and for special occasions such as "Blessing Before Moving from a Home" and "Blessing Near the Time of Birth."

• *Scripture study program* • Look into establishing a family Scripture study program at your parish like the *Little Rock Scripture Study Program* (The Liturgical Press), which now has a Children's Study. Parents and children meet separately to study a book of the Bible and then throughout the week pray and carry out activities related to that book.

Gimmicks
as Prayer Starters

Pray without ceasing. 1 Thessalonians 5:17

People learn to swim in different ways. Some begin by doing the dog paddle. Others learn to swim with the aid of an inner tube. Some people are simply thrown into deep water and swim to save their lives.

Praying, too, can be learned by means of different, sometimes novel, techniques. The activities in this chapter serve as a boost into prayer. Although they may be regarded as gimmicks, they have value in that they grab the students' attention and at the same time let them get their feet wet in the art of prayer.

• *Add-a-word* • Go around the class round-robin style, each student adding one word to a prayer. Or create a popcorn prayer by letting students anywhere in the room add a phrase spontaneously.

• *Add-a-(written) word* • Have each row or group of students circulate a sheet of paper on which each one adds a few words to compose a prayer.

• *Alphabetic prayer* • Here is a good suggestion for filling in the time of waiting during a class reconciliation: Tell the students to take each letter of the alphabet, think of a word for it, and then make up a prayer with that word. Example:

A - animals: Thank you, God, for all the unique animals you have put in this world. You must be very clever.

B - baby sister: Jesus, please keep my baby sister from harm.

• *Filling a need* • Invite students to write prayers in order to fill a need: part of a school campaign for right-to-life, a prayer corner in the parish bulletin, school prayers over the public address system during Advent, a prayer service for Mother's Day, and so on.

• *Acrostics* • Have the students create acrostics in which each letter of a word begins a phrase or line of the prayer. The word may be the name of a person or the subject of the prayer. Example:

Because you love me, God,
In your infinite goodness and mercy,
By your gift of the Bible you
Lead me to
Everlasting life with you. Thank you!

• *Finish a prayer* • Read aloud an incomplete prayer, pausing to let the students supply words aloud or in their hearts. Example:

O God, most _____,
I thank you for _____ and _____.
Please help me to _____ and to be more _____.
I pray for _____ that he or she may _____.
I ask this in the name of Jesus. Amen.

• *Food for thought* • Tell the students to choose a food that is a symbol for themselves. Let them draw or make the food out of art materials and then write a prayer about it. Example: Pizza

Jesus, I am like pizza.
I'm usually where people are having a good time.
You have given me gifts that make others happy:
    quick wit, like spicy sausage;
    gentleness, like soft mushrooms;
    loyalty to friends, like sticky cheese;
    and common sense, like bread.
Thank you for making me the unique combination that I am.

• *Short prayers* • Have the students compose short prayers that might be used for dial-a-prayer or for a radio spot.

• *Doodle prayers* • Distribute art paper and have students draw a looped design without lifting their pencils from the paper. Tell them to find a figure in their abstract art and color it. Then have them write a prayer based on that figure.

• *Prayers from designs* • Drop food coloring or water colors on a transparency. Tape another sheet to the top and press down. Have the students find a topic for prayer in the picture.

• *Prayers from music* • Play a piece of music, religious or secular, and have the students respond with a written personal prayer.

• *Prayers for personal wishes* • Invite the students to make a personal wish list. Guide them to write what is close to their heart and not ridiculous things. Have them star the three wishes that mean the most to them and write prayers of petition for these.

• *Prayers in advertising space* • Ask the students to pretend that they have the job of composing a prayer for a billboard, a magazine or newspaper page, a sign in a bus, or the back of a cereal box. Direct them to write a prayer that would be appropriate for people today.

• *Prayers from three objects* • Have the students bring in three unrelated things, or pictures of them, and write a prayer based on their objects. For example, someone who brings in a bear, a watch, and make-up might write: "Jesus, please *bear* with me and *watch* over me. I want to *make up* for my sins."

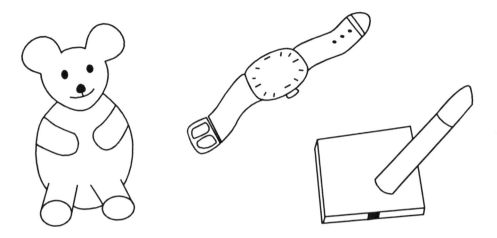

• *Titles of Jesus* • Let the students choose a title of Jesus and write a prayer about it. Have them invent a crismon of the title and decorate their paper with it. A crismon is a symbol for Christ. The word comes from the words *Christ* and *monogram*. Possible titles:

Son of God	Messiah	Son of Mary	way
Christ	Word of God	Son of Man	truth
Savior	rabbi	Prince of Peace	life
Redeemer	prophet	Alpha and Omega	
Lord	king	Light of the World	
Lamb of God	Good Shepherd	Sacred Heart	
Master	Son of David	Bread of Life	
Emmanuel	suffering servant	risen Lord	

• *Four directions* • Have the students work in four groups to compose a prayer for each direction: north, south, east, and west. Pray their prayers together, facing each direction in turn.

• *The passion and death of Jesus* • Tell the students to write a reflective prayer as if they were a person or an object that figured in the suffering and death of Jesus.

• *Knotted prayers* • Distribute strips of paper and have the students write a prayer of love to God. Tell them to tie the strip in a knot with the prayer inside and take the "love-knot" home as a reminder of their love for God.

• *Displayed prayers* • Have the students write prayers on leaves or flowers and hang them on a tree or write prayers on hearts or diamonds and post them on a bulletin board.

• *Patterns* • Let the students choose a color or a number and compose a prayer based on it. Or have them write prayers connected to many colors (like the colors of a rainbow or of jelly beans), or the numbers from one to ten or twelve, or a deck of playing cards.

• *National Day of Prayer* • Do something special to commemorate National Day of Prayer, the first Thursday of May, which was signed into law by President Ronald Reagan.

• *Putting together a prayer* • Present the following chart to the students. Have them choose a term or phrase from each column to compose a one-sentence prayer that fits them. Suggest that they use their prayer as a mantra, repeating it in their hearts.

Title for God		Title for Self		Ending	
Dear	God	your sinful	son	needs	help
Heavenly	Father	your frightened	daughter	begs for	advice
Gentle	Son	your confident	child	thanks you for	forgiveness
Kind	Spirit	your fearful	creature	asks for	you
Forgiving	Creator	your sorrowful	brother	longs for	courage
Loving	Jesus	your grateful	sister	appreciates	confidence
Just	Christ	your confused	servant	enjoys	faith
Mysterious	Savior	your joyful		pleads for	your goodness
Unseen	Redeemer	your eager		has	patience
Merciful	Friend	your angry		adores	peace
Powerful	Protector	your loving		searches	for an answer
Faithful	Judge	your struggling		hopes for	understanding
All wise	Master	your determined		fears	friendship
Patient	Brother	your lonely		loves	strength
Almighty	Guide	your faithful		praises	generosity
Infinite	Lord	your worried		trusts	love

Hymns and Poems

Then, after singing a hymn, they went out to the Mount of Olives.

Mark 14:26

Tagore said, "God respects me when I work, but loves me when I sing." Augustine declared that singing is praying twice. In song we give voice to thoughts and emotions that lie deep in our soul. No wonder then that prayer is sometimes sung. The music intimately joined to worship comes in various forms: Gregorian chant, solid Protestant hymns, Black spirituals, guitar songs, and soft rock. A wise catechist sees that music plays a part in religion lessons.

Hymns as Prayer

• *Lesson activities* • Have the students listen to or sing a religious song to open or close a class or to develop or reinforce a lesson.

• *The chorus* • Play a song and have students join in only with the chorus.

• *Teaching hymns* • Teach hymns sung at parish liturgies. Use this procedure:

   1. Have the students listen to the song.
   2. Discuss the words.
   3. Have the students hum along to the song.
   4. Sing or play a line at a time and have the students repeat it.
   5. Have the class sing the entire song.
   6. Go over any rough spots.

• *Analysis of lyrics* • Prepare questions that make the students delve into the meaning of a song's lyrics, discussing them with the whole class or in groups.

• *Illustrations* • Direct the students to illustrate a favorite line of a song, or have groups of students each make a poster for an assigned line.

• *Background music* • While the students do quiet work, play religious songs softly in the background.

• *Taizé prayer* • Introduce your students to the slow, reflective, sung prayers of the monks of Taizé. Their music is available on cassettes.

• *A prayer service* • Plan a prayer service on a certain theme with songs that have that theme: faith, hope, justice, presence of God, discipleship.

• *Gestures* • Teach gestures to a song or have the students invent them. You might have them sign a song using the language of the deaf.

• *Dance* • Let the students create a liturgical dance for a song.

• *Slides* • Help the students find slides to accompany a religious song as a prayer experience for a special occasion.

• *Original songs* • Challenge the students to write their own original song or write original words to a familiar melody.

• *Doctrine from hymns* • Have the students study hymns in order to learn church teachings. At Pentecost, for example, let them analyze the Sequence and other hymns to the Holy Spirit. This activity will make them more conscious of the words they sing during the liturgy.

• *Popular songs* • Older students will enjoy discovering that some popular songs have religious themes or can be easily applied to religion. When an older Sister I know thought she was alone with Jesus in chapel, she used to sing love songs from her era.

• *Planning music for Mass* • Give the students opportunities to choose the hymns for a celebration of the Eucharist.

Poems as Prayer
• *Examples* • Use poetry that is prayer. Here are two of my favorites. The first is "High Flight" by John Gillespie Magee, Jr.

> Oh! I have slipped the surly bonds of earth
>   And danced the skies on laughter-silvered wings;
> Sunward I've climbed, and joined the tumbling mirth
>   Of sun-split clouds—and done a hundred things
> You have not dreamed of—wheeled and soared and swung
>   high in the sunlit silence. Hov'ring there,
> I've chased the shouting wind along, and flung
>   My eager craft through footless halls of air.
>
> Up, up the long, delirious, burning blue
>   I've topped the wind-swept heights with easy grace,
> Where never lark, or even eagle flew—
> And, while with silent, lifting mind I've trod
>   The high untrespassed sanctity of space,
> Put out my hand and touched the face of God.

And a poem by e.e. cummings:

> i thank You God for most this amazing
> day: for the leaping greenly spirits of trees
> and a blue true dream of sky; and for everything
> which is natural which is infinite which is yes
>
> (i who have died am alive again today,
> and this is the sun's birthday; this is the birth
> day of life and of love and wings: and of the gay
> great happening illimitably earth)
>
> how should tasting touching hearing seeing
> breathing any—lifted from the no
> of all nothing—human merely being
> doubt unimaginable You?
>
> (now the ears of my ears awake and
> now the eyes of my eyes are opened)

• *A collection* • Collect religious poems from books and magazines and use them to enrich your classes.

• *Memorizing* • Have your students memorize poems that are prayers. I've never forgotten the prayer I learned in the ninth grade:

> O God, I love you for yourself,
> And not that I may heaven gain,
> Nor because those who love you not
> Must suffer hell's eternal pain.
>
> You, O my Jesus, you did me
> Upon the cross embrace;
> For me did bear the nails and spear
> And manifold disgrace,
>
> And griefs and torments numberless,
> And sweat of agony,
> Even death itself—and all for one
> Who was your enemy.
>
> Then why, O blessed Jesus Christ,
> Should I not love you well?
> Not for the sake of winning heaven,
> Nor of escaping hell;

Not with the hope of gaining things,
Not seeking a reward;
But, as you yourself have loved me,
O ever-loving Lord.

And so I love you, and will love,
And in your praise will sing,
Solely because you are my God
And my eternal king.

• *Original poems* • Encourage the students to compose their own poem-prayers to God, to Mary, to the saints, and to their patron saints. Let them experiment with the many forms of poetry: couplets, ballads, elegies, sonnets, diamantes, cinquains, etc.

• *Catholic poets* • Introduce your class to Catholic poets like Gerard Manley Hopkins and Jessica Powers.

• *Interpretations* • Have the students write their interpretations of religious poems and illustrate them.

• *Slide show* • Let the students create a slide show to accompany a poem like the Magnificat.

See "R: Resources," page 76, for sources for songs.

Inspirational *Pieces*

Let my prayer come like incense before you. Psalm 141:2

Every now and then someone creates a wise saying, a reflection, a poem, or a story that has power to touch the hearts of many people. Such inspirational pieces find their way into magazines, books, and church bulletins. They are used in workshops and retreats and are passed from one person to another. In trying to bring students closer to God, it is helpful to collect such pieces and use them in class. Illustrations G-K, pages 121-126, are the five popular religious writings: "One Solitary Life," "Desiderata," "Footprints," "Letter from Jesus," and "Persons are Gifts."

This year I had an operation on my foot. As the doctors and nurses prepared for the surgery, one of the nurses commented, "We don't often have a patient who can talk. Tell us a story, Sister." So flat on my back, I told one of my favorite stories, "Tatterrags." Very simply, it's about a little boy in Italy who is too poor to have a costume for the annual town festival. His friends have colorful outfits. When the festival draws near, each boy cuts a piece from his costume and takes it to the poor boy's mother. Out of the pieces she sews a costume of many colors. The poor boy goes to the festival wearing the most wonderful costume because he is clothed in the love of his friends.

Here are some ways to use inspiring pieces in class:

• *Springboard for prayer* • Have the students choose a line or an idea from an inspirational piece and develop their own prayer from it.

• *Gifts* • Give copies of inspiring passages to students on their birthdays, for Christmas, or to mark other memorable occasions.

• *Special religious events* • Use inspiring pieces in retreats, days of recollection, or liturgical celebrations. Give the students copies as mementoes.

• *An entire lesson* • Occasionally devote a class session to an experience with an inspirational piece: Read it, discuss it, and let the students pray over it themselves.

• *Displaying quotations* • Display inspiring quotations in the classroom and change them frequently. Draw from your own collection or use a book such as *Bartlett's Book of Familiar Quotations.*

• *Passages in literature* • Read to the students, or have them read, beautiful significant passages in spiritual books and articles. Discuss and pray over the ideas presented.

• *Stories* • Incorporate stories into your lessons, like "The Three Hermits" in the Introduction to this book. You will be imitating Jesus who told stories to capture the minds and hearts of his listeners and lift them up to God. If possible, tell the stories instead of reading them aloud. Practice first. Good stories are found in the books of John Shea, Anthony de Mello, and Edward Hays. Folk tales and stories from other countries can stimulate reflection and prayer. So can short films and videos.

• *Children's literature* • Many excellent children's books are available to read aloud and have the students respond to in prayer. *Love You Forever* by Robert Munsch, for instance, can be used to teach students of all ages about unconditional love. It tells about a mother's love for her son throughout her life. After she dies, the son shows the same lasting love for his daughter. Another children's book, *Brothers,* is a Jewish folk tale about two brothers who live on farms near each other. One brother has a family and the other isn't married. Every so often the married brother says to himself, "My brother is all alone while I have sons and daughters to take care of me. I am better off." During the night he carries grain to his brother's storehouse. Every so often the single brother says to himself, "My brother has a family to feed and care for. I am better off." And during the night, he carries grain to his brother's storehouse. One night the two brothers meet. The town planted a tree to mark the place where they met.

• *Lives of the Saints* • St. Ignatius owed his conversion to reading the lives of the saints. Inspire your students with true-life stories, including your own.

• *Drama* • Have the students present inspirational stories as dramatic readings or plays to another class, parents, or parishioners and end with a short prayer service.

• *Original pieces* • Invite your students to write their own inspiring pieces and share them with the class: a meditation on a burning candle, or thoughts during a thunderstorm or at the oceanside, even a story from their lives.

Jesus
and Prayer

Lord, teach us to pray. Luke 11:1

We can learn much about prayer from the greatest pray-er of all: Jesus. As truly human, Jesus shared our need for prayer. He prayed to his Father, Abba. Not only is Jesus a model for us, but he gave us guidelines for prayer and also presented us with the most loved prayer, the Our Father.

Jesus as Model and Teacher of Prayer

• *Jesus' prayer in Scripture* • Have the students locate times when Jesus prayed and summarize how, where, and when he prayed. You might use the following references. Let the students play disciples being interviewed about Jesus' prayer.

> Matthew 11:25
> Mark 1:35
> Luke 4:16
> Luke 6:12
> Luke 22:31-32
> Luke 22:39-42
> John 17:1-26

• *Imagined prayers* • Ask the students to imagine and write the prayers Jesus prayed to his Father on different days of his life.

• *Jesus' teaching* • Have the students locate the following references and read Jesus' advice for praying.

> Matthew 6:5-6   Luke 18:9-14
> Matthew 6:9-13   Luke 20:47
> Matthew 7:21-23   Luke 21:34-38
> Luke 11:5-8   Luke 22:39
> Luke 17:11-19   John 16:23
> Luke 18:2-8

• *Prayer lab* • Hold a two-day prayer lab called "Learning Prayer from the Master" from the blackline masters in Illustration L, pages 127-128. Arrange the students into six groups and distribute copies of the lab sheets. Assign each group a task from one to six. Have them proceed in order from task to task so that each group fifteen minutes for each task. At the end of the experience, evaluate the activity as a class. Ask questions like the following:

1. Did you enjoy this experience?
2. What concept about prayer struck you the most?
3. Which task did you find most helpful?
4. What would have made the lab more effective?

The Prayer Lab may be used as a contract assignment that the students do at home. They may contract for the following grades for activities that are well done:

6 activities   A
5 or 4 activities   B
3 or 2 activities   C
1 activity   D

Use any of the activities in the prayer lab as a whole class activity.

The Lord's Prayer

• *Gestures* • Teach or let the students make up gestures for the Our Father.

• *Reflecting* • Pray the Our Father with the class, pausing after every word or so to give the students time to reflect.

• *Song* • Teach a sung version of the Our Father.

• *Meditations* • Divide the class into groups and assign each group a line from the Our Father. Have each group write a meditation on their line.

• *Slides* • Help the class prepare a slide presentation to accompany the Our Father.

• *A mural* • Have the class plan and make a mural on the Our Father with a group assigned to do art for each phrase of the prayer.

• *Modern interpretation* • Like all of Scripture, the Our Father can be interpreted in the context of modern times. Have the class write an interpretation of this prayer in light of what is occurring in their world today.

Kinds of *Prayer*

Pray at every opportunity in the Spirit. Ephesians 6:18

Students, like all of us, learn to pray best by praying. Do not overwhelm them with words about praying. Take them directly to God through prayer. The time you provide in class may be the only time the students pray. There are multiple forms and styles of prayer. They vary from person to person and may change from day to day for an individual. In class let the students explore the various forms of prayer that enrich our Catholic tradition. Encourage the students to try them at home.

• *Explanation* • Tell the students that the forms and styles of prayer are like many pathways to God. Present a basic principle in the spiritual life: Pray as you can, not as you can't. Explain that prayer preferences change. Some appeal now and some don't. Some that don't appeal now may appeal next year. Tell the students that it is good to know how to pray different ways, so that they are ready for their future tastes. Who knows? They might even be able to guide someone else in prayer.

• *Shared experiences* • Invite the students to tell about ways they have prayed.

• *Varying prayers* • Begin class with different types of prayer, or use them as responses during class and at the end.

• *Prayer leaders* • Let the students take turns being prayer leaders or captains for class prayers. They might plan a daily prayer themselves. Challenge them to be unique, like the girl who, arms outstretched, called down God's blessing.

• *Ready-made prayers* • Use the ready-made prayers of saints or others. These borrowed prayers often express well what is in our hearts.

• *Favorite prayers* • Let the students share favorite prayers. Share yours. Here is part of one of mine, the prayer of Elizabeth of the Trinity:

> O Holy Trinity, whom I adore, help me to forget myself completely, so that I may establish myself in you, changeless and calm, as though my soul were already in eternity. May nothing disturb my peace, nor estrange me from you. At every moment may I penetrate further into the depths of your mystery.

• *Prayer booklet* • Have the students compile a prayer booklet or give them one. This is one sheet of paper with prayers typed so that when it's folded, it forms a four-page booklet. Use two sheets of paper to make an eight-page prayer booklet. See Illustration M, pages 129-130, for suggested prayers for a booklet for older students.

• *Prayer pocket* • Display a prayer pocket in the classroom to hold prayer cards the students have lettered and designed. The students can use these prayers to start religion class or pray them individually during free moments.

• *Religious articles* • Ask the students to bring a religious article from home. Discuss it and how it can lead us to prayer. Then set it in the prayer corner.

• *Variety in Jesus' prayer* • Discuss how Jesus prayed many types of prayers. He prayed with his community in the Temple. He blessed the children. He prayed alone on the mountain and in the desert. He prayed aloud in the presence of others several times. He sang psalms at the Last Supper.

Meditation

There are different methods for using the imagination to facilitate prayer. In his journal Wordsworth recorded that when he was in a beautiful place, he often imagined Jesus next to him—for instance, when he wrote his poem "Daffodils." Provide the time and quiet during religion class for your students to enjoy meditation.

• *Quieting little children* • Settle them down by having them make the Sign of the Cross lightly on their foreheads over and over until Jesus is in their minds.

• *Imagining Jesus* • Suggest to the students that they imagine Jesus sitting next to them or on an empty chair in their room. Tell them to speak to him aloud softly and imagine what he says in reply. After they have tried this at home, ask them to share their reactions to the prayer experience. Invite smaller children to imagine that Jesus is holding their hand and they are tiptoeing into a special place with him. Then have them think of themselves with him. For instance, have them imagine that they are in the crowd of children that runs to Jesus, or next to him in a boat, or sitting in his lap, or walking down a road with him.

• *A heart room* • Once I was in an audience of a thousand people when Father George Maloney took us in an imaginary elevator down into the depths of our hearts. He slowly called out the floors as we descended, then left us in silence to commune with God. Sister Marlene Halpin suggests that children invite God into their heart and then give him a tour of it. Sister Mary Terese Donze leads children to pray "in their heart room" where God is. She bases her meditations on an object or picture. First she presents an object and has the students consider its characteristics. Then she reflects on it, relating it to life. Finally, she draws the children into a conversation with Jesus.

• *A special place* • Explain to the students that some people pray by imagining a room, furnished to suit their taste ... rocking chair, fireplace, view of mountains out the window. They go into this room and meet Jesus there. Others withdraw mentally to a seashore, a garden, or a mountaintop. Let the students experiment with different settings.

• *Wonder and prayer* • Invite the students to recall a time when they experienced God's love for them in a special way, when they felt close to God. Have them recall the place, the details of what happened, and how they felt. Then tell them to re-live that event in their imagination. Finally, have them speak to God about it.

• *Ignatian meditation* • Teach the students to meditate on a Gospel event in the manner presented by St. Ignatius in the *Spiritual Exercises:*

1. Ask for a particular grace.
2. Use your imagination and senses to fill in the details of the setting, hear and see the characters speak, and watch the action. Replay the event in your mind as if you were a participant. For instance, as you meditate on the Nativity, Mary might let you hold the newborn baby for a while.
3. Then discuss the event with Jesus.

• *Guided meditations* • Sister Jane Reehorst, B.V.M., has written three books of guided meditations for students that flow from Scripture. See "R: Resources," page 76.

• *Fantasy prayer* • The previous paragraphs describe a meditation based on Scripture in which we participate in an event in Christ's life and then talk about it with him. A type of fantasy prayer similar to this is based not on a Gospel event but on symbolism. Create a symbolic situation in which the students imagine themselves there, make choices, act and react, and then analyze their feelings. For example, they can imagine that they meet Jesus and he gives them a gift. What will he give them? Why? How do they react? *Imagine That!* by Sister Marlene Halpin, O.P., contains samples of fantasies for children. You can also create them yourself.

• *Jesus by your side* • Propose to the students a way that St. Teresa recommends to experience the Risen Lord: Imagine that Jesus is by your side all during the day. Communicate with him every so often, with or without words.

• *Sharing meditations* • Invite the students to share their meditation experiences, but do not force them.

See Illustration N, page 131, for one effective meditation experience.

Contemplation
Contemplation is simply resting in God, peacefully placing your attention on God. Think of the word as being made up of the Latin *con*, which means "with" and the word for "temple." To contemplate is to be with God a sacred place, in the temple. In this case, the temple is ourselves.

• *Preparation* • Some Christians find it helpful to use exercises from oriental religions not only for relaxing but for entering the contemplative state. Anthony de Mello described a number of these exercises at length in *Sadhana: A Way to God.* You might give your students a taste of them. Here are a few of these exercises that help us grasp God beyond thoughts and images:

1. Keep silent and become aware of your mind. What is revealed to you?
2. Become aware of body sensations. Move from one part of your body to another, becoming conscious of the sensations in it.
3. Become aware of your breathing. Be aware of the air as it passes through your nostrils. Realize that the air you are breathing is filled with the presence of God. As you breathe, you are drawing God in.
4. Become aware of the sounds around you. Be aware of your power to hear. Realize that God is sounding all around you.
5. Take a familiar object and hold it. Use all your senses to become fully aware of it.

Spontaneous Prayer

• *Being sensitive* • When it comes to spontaneous prayer, a lot of us suddenly get lockjaw. Help your students with spontaneous prayer. Give them confidence by letting them first write their personal prayers. Then invite them to participate, asking, "Is anyone willing to?" or "Does anyone wish to?" Never pressure a student to share prayer.

• *Building confidence* • Ease your students into spontaneous prayer by having them write anonymous prayers on slips of paper. Put the slips in a prayer bag and pass it around. Have each student draw a slip and pray the prayer on it.

• *Prayers from pictures* • Paste pictures on a bottle or a carton and pass it around, inviting each student to say a simple prayer based on one of the pictures.

Vocal Prayer

• *Varying methods* • Pray prepared prayers in different ways:

1. Let the whole class pray aloud.
2. Divide the class into sides to alternate praying parts of the prayer.
3. Divide the class into groups and have them each pray part of the prayer.
4. Pray the prayer yourself and have the class join silently in their hearts.
5. Pray one phrase of a prayer at a time and have the students echo it.
6. Prepare a student or two to pray the prayer aloud.
7. Appoint a leader for litanies and intercessions. Direct the class to respond.
8. Play soft background music during vocal prayer.
9. Set up a prayer as a choral reading like the *Te Deum* is arranged in Illustration O, page 132.

Informal Prayer

• *Being a model* • Be a model for your students in praying informally. Pray aloud about daily classroom occurrences or world situations. For instance at the first snowfall, praise God for his beautiful gifts of creation; and when a fire engine sounds, offer a brief prayer for the persons who are in danger.

• *Eliciting prayer* • Elicit informal prayers from the class at various points during a lesson. For instance, after telling the story of the Last Supper comment, "Let's thank Jesus now for giving us this gift of the Eucharist. I'll start. Thank you, Jesus, for your great love."

Communal Prayer

• *Celebrations* • Hold celebrations with song, Scripture, litanies, shared petitions, traditional prayers, and actions. Little children especially need to express their prayer with their bodies. Prayer celebrations are not a waste of time but an opportunity for students to assimilate what they are learning. Celebrations allow mysteries to sink in, and they build community.

• *Conversational prayer* • Rosalind Rinker teaches "conversational prayer." In this form of shared prayer, people stand and pray aloud together to Jesus as a child would pray. With the guidance of the Holy Spirit, the participants engage in a personal conversation with Jesus following these four steps:

1. *Jesus is here.* Focus on Jesus and welcome him, audibly and silently. Praise him.
2. *Thank you, Lord.* Thank Jesus for the persons standing with you, calling them by name. Thank the Lord for specific gifts.
3. *Help me, Lord.* Be honest and specific. Pray for yourself.
4. *Help my brother and sister, Lord.* Pray for each person by name. Give thanks when someone prays for you. Pray for others.

See "R: Resources," page 76, for information about Rinker's book, *Learning Conversational Prayer.*

• *Faith sharing* • Below is a format for a faith-sharing session based on Scripture that could be used for a passage from one of the Sunday readings. Participants in a faith-sharing session pray over a passage individually before coming to the meeting. Students could read and pray over the passage as Thursday night's homework and then meet in small groups during class on Friday.

1. Prayer to the Holy Spirit and opening prayer by the leader.
2. Reading of the prepared passage and silence.
3. Comments on the passage.
4. Second reading of the passage and silence.
5. Sharing of how the passage addresses the participants personally.
6. Third reading of the passage.

7. Spontaneous prayer.
8. Concluding prayer: a prayer, the Our Father, a blessing, or a hymn.

Spiritual Reading
St. Benedict taught his monks a method of praying from Scripture called *lectio divina* (divine reading). It has three steps: *lectio* (reading), *meditatio* (meditation), and *oratio* (prayer). By absorbing the Word of God this way, we let it shape who we are and what we hope to be. This method of reading and praying can be applied to spiritual works other than the Bible.

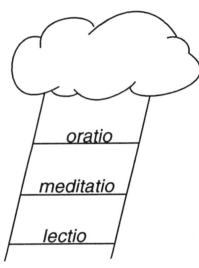

• *The steps* • Teach lectio divina to your students with or without the Latin words. (Some students will find the strange language intriguing.) Present the steps on a three-rung ladder going into the clouds.

1. Give your students a passage from the Bible. (Epistles are good for this type of reading.) Direct them to read until they find an idea that appeals to them.
2. Have the students pause and mull over the striking idea, repeating it over and over and letting it sink into their minds and hearts, delving into the meaning of the words and savoring them.
3. Invite them to speak with God about the passage. Tell them that when they are finished, they should return to the reading and repeat the process.

Charismatic Prayer
Teach the students about charismatic prayer, a free and spontaneous form of prayer usually experienced by people who have undergone what is known as baptism of the Holy Spirit. The Holy Spirit is present to them in a special way, and they pray with great joy in words that are unrecognizable. This prayer, the gift of tongues, often occurs when people who are called charismatic gather to pray together.

• *Guest speaker* • Invite someone who is familiar with charismatic prayer to be a guest speaker in your class.

• *Literature* • Read or encourage the students to read articles and books about charismatic prayer.

Movement
Prayer involves our whole being. Antal Dorati, the former conductor of the Washington National Symphony Orchestra, said in an interview: "I imagine that the first dance was a movement of adoration...the body simply moving to give thanks to the creator."

• *Gestures to a prayer* • Create, or have the students create, gestures to a prayer like the Our Father or the Magnificat.

• *Gestures to a song* • Have the students spontaneously create movements to a song as a form of prayer. All the class can participate if there is enough space so that individuals don't interfere with one another's prayer.

• *Original dances* • Let one student or a small group invent and teach a dance to the class.

• *Enhancing the Mass* • Add liturgical movement to a song in order to enhance a Eucharistic celebration.

• *Cheers* • Invent or have the student invent cheers like the following Easter cheer for small children:

Jesus is risen.
[Take two steps forward on the beats.]
Alleluia!
[Raise arms up and down twice on the beats.]
Jesus is risen.
[Take two steps backward.]
Alleluia!
[Raise arms up and down twice.]
Jesus is risen.
[Take two steps forward on the beats.]
Alleluia!
[Raise arms up and down twice.]
That's gr—rr—
[Swing right arm around twice as if winding up for a pitch.]
—eat!
[Jerk right elbow back. Clap twice.]

• *Pep rally* • If you are ambitious, have your class organize a holy pep rally. Groups of students from different grade levels perform and lead cheers to celebrate and honor God. Other topics to cheer about include Jesus, the Holy Spirit, Mary, the saints, the church, and the gift of life.

• *Processions and parades* • Hold processions as part of prayer services. Explain that prayerfully moving from one place to another is a form of worship. Ask the students to identify the three processions in the celebration of Eucharist (the entrance procession, the procession with the gifts, and the Communion procession). Ask them if they know of other times when we process in church (Passion Sunday, Forty Hours). Have the students make banners for their processions or carry other things. Small children may have "parades" instead of processions: a Mary parade, a saint parade, a praise parade.

One-liners

Prayers can be very short. In fact, my most frequent prayer is probably "Help!" Father Edward Hays muses that the oldest and shortest of all prayers was an expression of awe at the wonders of God's world. When our earliest ancestors saw green shoots breaking through Earth from seed, when they saw a rainbow, a sunrise, or a night sky spangled with stars, they responded, "O-h-h-h!"

• *Learning short prayers* • Teach the students to pray short prayers like "Jesus, Mary, Joseph" or "My God and my All." Have them print one-line prayers on drawing paper and make pictures for them.

• *A list* • Have the students call out as many one-line prayers as they can while two secretaries record them on the board.

• *Original one-liners* • Encourage the students to compose their own one-line prayers for situations like the following:

    Getting into a car
    During a storm
    Not being able to find something
    Beholding a beautiful flower
    Being lost
    Realizing you hurt someone

Flag prayers

Have your students make flag prayers in the tradition of the Tibetan Buddhists. Explain that a prayer flag is set outside so that breezes can carry the prayer on it to

heaven. Distribute pieces of material, sticks or dowels, and permanent markers. Tell the students to think of a prayer word or short phrase that they would like to pray, such as "Peace" or "Alleluia." Have them letter this prayer on the material and add art if they wish. Direct the students to fasten the material to the dowel with staples, tape, or string to make a flag that stands in the ground or one that hangs down like a banner. Encourage them to set up the flag at home.

A variant of this is to have the students letter prayers on small pieces of smooth wood. These prayer sticks then could be burned to represent offering the prayers to God.

See the following chapters: "C: Centering Prayer," page 19; "E: Eucharist: the Greatest Prayer," page 27; "L: Liturgical Prayer," page 53; and "R: Resources," page 76.

Liturgical Prayer

Where two or three are gathered together in my name, there am I in the midst of them.
Matthew 18:20

Liturgical prayer is our public prayer when we assemble as a community to profess and celebrate what we believe. We praise, thank, ask pardon, and petition God as one body. Participating in this prayer strengthens our bonds with God and with one another. It makes us grow in divine life and all forms of love. During liturgical prayer, the secular and the sacred meet. Through words, actions, and symbols we connect with God and become more like God.

It is essential for catechists to prepare students to join fully with God's people as they pray in the liturgy: the Eucharist, the Prayer of Christians (the Divine Office), and the sacraments. Not only must students know the meaning of these rituals, they should find them a solid source of nourishment for their lives. The following ideas and those in "E: Eucharist—the Greatest Prayer," will foster an understanding and love for liturgical prayer.

Liturgy of the Hours: Christian Prayer
• *Praying one of the hours* • Introduce your students to a brief form of one of the hours. You might pray morning prayer together to celebrate a certain occasion.

• *The structure* • Give the students an outline of one of the hours and explain it to them. Here is the format for Morning Prayer:

> *Lord, open my lips. (Sign a cross on your lips.)*
> *And my mouth shall proclaim your praise.*
> *Glory to …*

> Antiphon
> Psalm with a Glory Be and a short prayer

> Antiphon
> Canticle from Scripture with a Glory Be and a short prayer

> Antiphon
> Psalm with a Glory Be and a short prayer

Reading from Scripture
Responsory

Antiphon
Zechariah's Canticle
Antiphon repeated

Intercessions
Our Father

Prayer of the day
May the Lord bless us, protect us from all evil, and bring us to everlasting life. Amen.

• *History of the Liturgy of the Hours* • Present the history of the Liturgy of the Hours and its role in the church today.

• *In lessons* • Use parts of a day's hours in your lessons. For instance, end a lesson about Mary with the intercessions from the common of the Blessed Virgin Mary.

Paraliturgical Services
• *Culminating activities* • End units with celebrations that incorporate meaningful rituals. Involve as many students as possible.

• *Significant events* • Celebrate important world, school, and calendar events with prayer services.

• *Music* • Play background music as rituals are being carried out in class or school prayer services.

• *Original services* • Let the students plan a paraliturgical service. Possible topics: discipleship, love, witness, faith, Mary, creation, hope, life, heaven, God's law, the Beatitudes. Incorporate rituals and symbols. See a paraliturgical prayer service on Christian service in Illustration P, pages 133-134.

Sacraments
• *Class participation* • Participate in the sacraments as a class if possible.

• *Prayers of the sacraments in lessons* • Incorporate prayers from the rituals of the sacraments into your lessons.

• *Symbols of the sacraments in prayer services* • Use the symbols of the sacraments in other prayer services in different ways. For instance, plan a prayer service on oil or on keeping the commandments that includes blessing the students with holy oil.

• *Guest speakers* • Invite people who have just experienced a sacrament and ministers of the sacraments to be guest speakers in your class.

• *Christ's work* • Link the sacraments with Christ's life on earth. Show how each sacrament is an extension of his work today.

• *Symbol study* • Plan an in-depth study of one of the sacramental symbols. For instance, show a movie about water, distribute cups of cold water to drink, invite the students to share good and bad experiences with water, use a globe or map to illustrate how much water is on earth, invite a scientist to speak about the importance of water for life, or take the class swimming! Have the class write poems about water and draw pictures of its uses. Culminate with a prayer service that has water for the theme and includes blessing the students with holy water.

• *Hymns* • Study hymns that are appropriate for each sacrament.

• *Booklets* • Have the students make an illustrated booklet about one of the sacraments, explaining the sacrament's importance, the symbols that are used in it, and the prayers.

• *Mobiles* • Divide the class into seven groups and have each group make a mobile or poster for a sacrament.

Sacrament of Penance (Reconciliation)

• *Group preparation* • Prepare your students for the celebration of this sacrament together as a class.

• *Gospel passages* • Meditate on a Gospel passage that shows God's merciful love:

Good Shepherd	Luke 15:1-7
Sinful Woman	John 8:3-11
Anointing at Bethany	Luke 7:36-50
Prodigal Son	Luke 15:11-24
Zacchaeus	Luke 19:1-8

• *Examination of conscience* • Help the students examine their consciences. Let them consider their thoughts and actions at home, in school, and in the neighborhood. You might have them write their own examinations of conscience.

• *During a class celebration* • Provide prayer sheets or booklets to occupy the students as they wait for the class to finish receiving the sacrament.

• *A closing ritual* • Use a ritual to symbolize the conversion that has taken place. For example when the students come out of the reconciliation room or confessional, have them hang paper or clay hearts on a tree or post a piece of a rainbow onto a large pattern.

• *A party* • Celebrate the sacrament with a party afterwards.

• *A family celebration* • Sponsor a family reconciliation day.

Marian
Prayer and Prayer to the Saints

They have no wine. John 2:3

The greatest Christian prayer is prayer to the Father through the Son in the Holy Spirit. For two thousand years Christians have also found it beneficial to turn to Mary, the Mother of God, and to other saints, asking their prayers and help.

The church prays to Mary as its mother and mediator. It was she who was closest to Jesus on earth. She was present at his birth in Bethlehem and his death on Calvary. She prompted his first miracle when a young couple was in need. Mary drew the Spirit down at the Annunciation and at Pentecost. When we ask a favor of Mary, we know we have a powerful intercessor. When we honor this wonderful, faith-filled woman, we honor God, who filled her with grace.

The church prays to the saints as fellow members in the Communion of Saints. Those people who have lived as disciples of Jesus on Earth, loving God and others as he did, now in heaven are in an even better position to help others for the glory of God.

Prayers to Mary and the saints have always held a role in church tradition. Young people should be acquainted with these prayers and encouraged to pray their own. They ought to know and take advantage of the fact that in heaven they have a mother and a host of friends.

Marian Prayer
• *Mary's feasts* • Introduce your students to Mary's feast days. Celebrate them when you can:

January 1	Solemnity of Mary, Mother of God
February 11	Our Lady of Lourdes
March 25	Annunciation of the Lord
May 13	Our Lady of Fatima
May 31	Visitation
July 16	Our Lady of Mount Carmel
August 15	Assumption
August 22	Queenship of Mary
September 8	Birth of Mary
September 15	Our Lady of Sorrows
October 7	Our Lady of the Rosary
November 21	Presentation of Mary

| December 8 | Immaculate Conception |
| First Saturday after the feast of the Sacred Heart | Immaculate Heart of Mary |

• *Mary's month and day* • Suggest that your students do something special to honor Mary during May, her month, and on Saturday, her day.

• *Marian prayers* • Explain the words of time-honored Marian prayers and encourage the students to memorize them: the Hail Mary, Angelus, Regina Coeli, Memorare, Consecration to Mary, and Litany of Loreto.

• *The Magnificat* • Teach the students Mary's prayer, the Magnificat, perhaps a sung version. Consider the meaning it has for us today.

• *The rosary* • Pray the rosary with the students. See "N: Noteworthy Prayers," page 60.

• *Mary's apparitions* • Tell the stories of Marian apparitions at Lourdes, Fatima, Guadalupe, and other places.

• *A pilgrimage* • Make a pilgrimage to a Marian shrine. Or take your class on a pilgrimage to statues or pictures of Mary on your parish property, praying a decade of the rosary at each stop.

• *Pictures* • Present pictures of Mary, such as Our Lady of Perpetual Help and Our Lady of Guadalupe. Discuss them and use them for reflection and prayer.

• *A May shrine* • During May set up a shrine to Mary in your classroom and suggest that the students make one at home.

• *A May crowning* • Hold a May crowning in your classroom, outside, or in church during which you sing hymns and pray to Mary.

• *Mary in Scripture* • Study Mary's appearances in Scripture and compose prayers to her based on them.
Luke 1:26-56	The annunciation
Luke 2:1-52	The visitation
John 2:1-12	The wedding at Cana
Mark 3:32-35	Calling for Jesus
John 19:25-27	The crucifixion

• *Office of Mary* • Pray parts of the Office of Mary from the Liturgy of the Hours in class.

• *Masses in honor of Mary* • Plan and celebrate Masses in honor of Mary.

• *A litany* • Have the students write their own litanies of Our Lady or write a prayer flowing from one of her titles in the Litany of Loreto.

• *Churches, people, and places* • Conduct a study of churches and shrines in honor of Mary. Guide the students to discover classmates' names and the names of well-known places that are derived from Mary and her role in our salvation.

• *Holy cards* • Distribute holy cards of Mary and use them as a focus for vocal or mental prayer. Have the students design personal holy cards of Mary.

• *Art masterpieces* • Show art masterpieces depicting scenes from Mary's life with narration in the form of a prayer.

• *Marian hymns* • Analyze the words of Marian hymns with the students and then sing them together.

• *Letter or poem* • Have the students write a letter or a poem to Mary and find or draw a picture to go with it.

• *"The Juggler of Our Lady"* • Tell the story "The Juggler of Our Lady," a French tale about a brother in a monastery who has no talent for anything except juggling. He juggles for Mary in the monastery chapel at night. One evening another monk sees him. That night the juggler collapses, exhausted, before Mary's statue. Mary herself appears and cares for the juggler.

• *Famous people devoted to Mary* • Study the lives of people who were devoted to Mary like St. Joseph, Louis de Montfort, St. Bernadette, Pope John XXIII, and Rev. Patrick Peyton.

• *Contemporary people* • Have the students find examples of people today who show devotion to Mary, such as Bob O'Bill, who had a 90-foot iron statue of Our Lady of the Rockies constructed in Montana.

Prayer to the Saints
• *Prayer to angels* • Teach the students the Prayer to St. Michael and the following updated version of the prayer to our Guardian Angel:

> **Prayer to the Guardian Angel**
> Angel sent by God to guide me,
> be my light and walk beside me;
> be my guardian and protect me;
> on the paths of life direct me.

• *All Saints Day* • Celebrate November 1 with Mass or a special prayer service. The students might dress as a chosen saint for the occasion.

• *Patron saints* • Have the students compose prayers, poems, or hymns to their patron saints.

• *Saint stories* • After presenting the life of a saint, pray the prayer from the Mass celebrated on his or her feast day.

• *Litany* • Pray the Litany of the Saints. You might add students' patron saints who are not included in the litany.

• *Original litany* • Have the students write a litany in honor of a particular saint.

• *Hymns* • Teach hymns in honor of the saints.

• *Daily saints* • Begin class with a summary of the life of the saint of the day and a prayer to him or her.

Noteworthy
Prayers

Ask and it will be given to you; seek and you will find;
knock and the door will be opened to you. Matthew 7:7

Teach traditional prayers and traditional devotions like the Way of the Cross, the rosary, Benediction, litanies, novenas, and visits. An eighty-year-old Sister I live with witnessed the power of the rosary when she was in the hospital. Her roommate was a seventy-year-old black woman. One day as Sister prayed her daily rosary, the woman asked if she would teach her how to pray it. Sister gave her her rosary. The woman then asked what she would have to do to become a Sister. Sister explained that she would have to become a Catholic first and then leave her husband. Believe it or not, the woman is taking instructions. I don't know if she plans to leave her husband. It all began with the rosary.

Traditional Prayers

Teach the Sign of the Cross, the Our Father, the Hail Mary, the Glory Be, the Apostles Creed, and an Act of Contrition.

• *Sign of the Cross* • In teaching the Sign of the Cross facing the children, use your left hand and move your hand from right to left so that when the children imitate you they make the Sign correctly. Explain that in this gesture we dedicate our entire being to the Trinity: mind (head), heart (chest), and whole life (shoulders).

• *Prayer listeners* • Invite parents, high school students, or retired sisters to be prayer listeners and hear your children pray the prayers while you are busy doing other things.

• *Awards* • Award children who can pray the prayers correctly without help. Give them stars, stickers, or a sign to wear—a blank nametag on which you have typed or written in large letters "I know the Our Father" (or other prayer being studied).

• *Teaching prayer formulas* • Here are some ways to teach the prayer formulas:

1. Write the phrases of a prayer to be learned on giant strips of multicolored paper that the children arrange in order and link together to form a chain. Or write the phrases on puzzle pieces that can be put together in order by the children as they pray the prayer. Make one large class puzzle and in-

2. Make a large circle on sturdy paper and mark off pie-shaped sections. In each section write a phrase from a prayer to be learned and attach a spinner to the center. The children spin the spinner, read the phrase pointed to, and add the next phrase.

3. Make two large circles. Divide one circle into pie-shaped sections and write phrases from a prayer in order in the sections. Cut a wedge out of the other circle the size of one of the sections. Attach this circle to the whole one with a brad. Have the children turn the top circle to reveal each consecutive phrase of a prayer in order to learn it. They can also turn the top circle to sections at random and see if they can say the phrase that follows the revealed phrase.

4. Make a wind-up card for a prayer. Print phrases from a prayer in mixed order along the two sides of a card. Print the entire prayer on the back of the card. Along the sides of the card make a notch next to each phrase. Cut a length of yarn or string so that the children can wind it around the card, going from phrase to phrase in the order of the prayer. Have them use the back of the card to check their work.

DOXOLOGY	
▶ is now	and to the ◀ Holy Spirit
▶ Glory	to the Father ◀
▶ and to the Son	in the ◀ beginning
▶ forever	and will be ◀
▶ as it was	Amen ◀

5. Divide a prayer into phrases and assign each phrase to a group of children. Have the group print the words on a sheet of paper with crayons or markers and draw symbols or illustrations to go with them. When the pictures are finished, tape them together to make a banner to hang in the room to help the children learn the prayer.

6. Make a transparency of a prayer to be learned, leaving blanks for some words. Have the children fill in the blanks.

7. Have the children bring in a box about the size of a 6-inch cube. Give each child copies of the traditional prayers to paste on each side of the cube. The children can keep these boxes in their rooms to help them learn the prayers and remember to pray.

8. Write the phrases of a prayer on cards of one color and interpretations of the phrases on cards of another color. Show the phrase cards and have the children match them.

Set 1	Set 2
Our Father	God made us and loves us.
Who art in heaven	Where God lives and all are happy
Hallowed be thy name	God's name is holy.
Thy kingdom come	May peace and love be everywhere.
Thy will be done	May everyone do what is good.
On earth as it is in heaven	May we live like saints.
Give us this day our daily bread	Give us what we need.
And forgive us our trespasses	Forgive us when we are bad.
As we forgive those who trepass against us	As we love people who hurt us.
And lead us not into temptation	Help us stay away from what might make us bad.
But deliver us from evil	Keep us safe.
Amen	Yes.

• *Songs* • Use song-versions of prayers in class.

• *Big books* • Have the children make a "big book" of a traditional prayer. Help them paste or draw pictures to illustrate different ideas in the prayer.

• *Interpretations* • Direct older students to do a line-by-line interpretation of familiar prayers, or do one yourself and share it with them.

The Rosary

• *Teaching the rosary* • Provide each student with a rosary and teach or review how to pray it. Display a poster of the rosary or a large diagram on the bulletin board. Give the students leaflets explaining how to pray the rosary and listing the mysteries.

• *Cord rosaries* • Teach the students to make cord rosaries and donate these to the missions. Your local chapter of the Legion of Mary can help you.

• *A class rosary* • Have the class work together to make a paper chain rosary.

• *History of the rosary* • Tell the history of the rosary.

• *A living rosary* • Form a living rosary in which each student represents a bead. The students lead the prayer for the bead they represent and place a flower in a vase near a statue or picture of Mary. The students representing the Our Fathers also announce the mystery and may give a brief reflection. For the Our Father beads, vigil lights may be used instead of flowers. Let the students read their parts from small papers so that apprehension doesn't spoil their prayer experience.

• *A worksheet* • Give the students a worksheet containing information about the rosary. See Illustration Q, page 135.

• *Drawings of the mysteries* • Have the students draw the mysteries of the rosary and display their drawings.

• *Drama* • Help the students act out each mystery of the rosary, dance it, or form a tableau of it.

• *The rosary in Mary's months* • Pray a decade of the rosary each day in May and October. Make a rosary chart and add beads each day as the students pray their way through the month.

• *Varying the rosary* • Teach the students ways to vary the praying of the rosary:

1. Create new Scripture-based mysteries of the rosary on certain topics, for instance, miracle mysteries or parable mysteries.

2. Concentrate on a different word or phrase of the Hail Mary for each decade.

3. Recall the decade's mystery by inserting a sentence about it between the two halves of the Hail Mary. Example:
   Hail Mary ... Jesus.
   (The Angel Gabriel appeared to you.)
   Holy Mary, Mother of God ... death. Amen.

4. Think of a different phase of the mystery for each bead of the decade.

Way of the Cross
• *Fridays of Lent* • Pray the stations with the students each Friday during Lent.

• *Booklets* • Give the students station booklets or have them make their own.

• *Reflections* • Have the students write a reflection on each station of the cross, relating the station to their concerns. The prayer for each station can take this form:
   1. Traditional opening: *We adore you, O Christ, and we bless you,*
      because by your holy cross you have redeemed the world.
   2. A sentence or two about the subject
   3. An application to the students' own lives
   4. A prayer of thanksgiving, petition, contrition, or love

• *Outdoor stations* • Pray an outdoor stations of the cross.

• *Shadow stations* • Have groups of students arrange themselves to represent each station behind a sheet with a light shining on them so that only their shadows are seen on the front of the sheet. Present the stations for another class or the parish.

• *Multimedia presentation* • Help the students work out the stations in a multimedia presentation incorporating modern music, dance, and drama.

Devotions to the Blessed Sacrament

• *Visits* • Foster in the students a habit of visiting the Blessed Sacrament by making class visits. Prepare the students for communal or personal prayer and then take them into the presence of the Blessed Sacrament.

• *Forty Hours* • Have the students participate in Forty Hours Devotion if your parish holds one.

• *St. John Neumann* • Tell how St. John Neumann introduced Forty Hours in the United States.

• *The Divine Praises* • Pray the Divine Praises with the students before the Blessed Sacrament. Invite them to add their own praises.

• *Saints* • Read your students the life of St. Tarcisius, St. Paschal Baylon, St. Gerard Majella, St. Clare, St. John Neumann, or another saint known for devotion to the Blessed Sacrament.

• *Prayer service* • Prepare, or have the students prepare, a prayer service of adoration of the Blessed Sacrament.

The Morning Offering

Teach your students to offer God everything they do throughout the day the first thing in the morning by praying the Morning Offering.

• *Offerings* • Discuss what kinds of things the students will be offering to God in union with the sacrifice of the Mass.

• *Intentions* • Obtain or make copies of the intentions of the Holy Father for each month. Encourage the students to keep their copy on their mirror or dresser.

• *A memory trick* • Suggest that the students place their shoes under the bed in the evening so the next morning when they kneel to get their shoes, they remember to pray. An alternate trick is to tie a sock around the bedpost. A "prayer rock" kept on the pillow and moved to the floor at night serves the same purpose.

Meal Prayers

• *Explanation* • Tell the students that praying before and after meals reminds us that everything we have is a gift from God, in particular our very life. We express our gratitude and pray for those who do not have a meal like ours.

• *Family meal prayers* • Help the students compose their own meal prayers which they can pray with their families. The best prayers can be made into a booklet for each student to take home to vary the prayers they say at meals.

• *Reminders* • Have the students make placecards or placemats with a short meal prayer on them for each member of their families.

Observances

This day shall be a memorial feast for you, which all your generations shall celebrate with pilgrimage to the LORD, as a perpetual institution.　　　Exodus 12:14

We Christians, like our Jewish ancestors in the faith, are a celebrating people. We commemorate great events and great people throughout the year. It's important to initiate youngsters into the meanings, rituals, customs, and prayers of feast days and seasons of the liturgical year. The celebrations that have evolved in the Christian community serve to bring home the Good News and enrich our spiritual lives. They keep our story alive.

• *Seasonal prayers* • Assign each student a season or a holiday for which to write an appropriate prayer. Compile the prayers into a book. If the book is well done, copies could be distributed to families in the parish.

Advent
• *Advent persons* • Begin each week with a prayer to one of the Advent figures:

Mary, the Mother of God, who waited nine months for Jesus
John the Baptist, who announced the coming of the Savior
Isaiah, a prophet whose prophecies of the Messiah are read during Advent

• *Class Advent wreath* • An Advent wreath reminds us that Christ is the Light of the World. Shape evergreens into a circle on a frame or coat hanger to represent that God is eternal. Set four candles in the wreath, preferably three purple candles and one pink to represent the third Sunday of Advent, Joyful Sunday. Add a bow at the base of each candle. If all white candles are used, the bows can be purple and pink. At the start of each week in Advent, light an additional candle and pray an Advent prayer. As an alternate, design a wreath on a bulletin board.

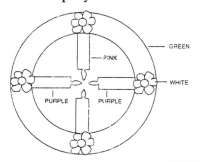

• *Individual Advent wreaths* • Have the students make their own Advent wreaths. They can draw one with four unlit candles or make one out of construction paper. They can construct an Advent wreath from a paper plate, cutting four lighted candles in the inner circle so that they are ready to be bent upright each week.

• *Living Advent wreaths* • Young children enjoy sitting in a circle to form a living Advent wreath. Four children stand to represent the candles.

• *Mary candle* • Make a Mary candle for the classroom during this season of waiting. Put an *M* with a chi-rho through it on a white candle using beads or felt. Tie blue ribbon around the candle and set it in greens with berries. Light it each week in Advent and pray to Mary.

• *Jesse tree* • Make a Jesse tree with symbols of people and events that led up to the coming of the Savior. Jesse, King David's father, is one of Jesus' ancestors. The tree can be a real tree, an artificial tree, an outline of a tree made with yarn on a bulletin board, or boxes stacked in the shape of a tree. Individuals can make any of the following symbols and compose prayers for them. Hold a ceremony in which the students explain their symbol, pray the prayer, and place the symbol on the tree.

> apple with two bites out of it (Adam and Eve)
> ark or rainbow (Noah)
> bundle of wood, ram in bush (Abraham and Isaac)
> pitcher (Rebecca)
> ladder (Jacob)
> well or coat of many colors (Joseph)
> burning bush or tablets of the Law (Moses)
> lamb on the altar (Paschal lamb)
> sword (Judith)
> sheaf of wheat (Ruth)
> root, stem, and flower or shepherd's staff (Jesse)
> harp, key, or crown and sceptre (David)
> Temple or scale of justice (Solomon)
> whale (Jonah)
> scroll (Isaiah)
> six-pointed star and chain (Esther)
> baptismal shell (John the Baptist)
> carpenter's tools: hammer, saw, chisel, angle, plane (Joseph)
> lily, crown circled by stars, or decorative *M* (Mary)
> city of Bethlehem, rising sun (Jesus)
> chi-rho placed on top of tree (Jesus the Savior)

• *"O" antiphons* • Teach the students about the "O" antiphons prayed in the Liturgy of the Hours and as the alleluia verse in Masses the seven days before Christmas. These recall what the prophets said of the Messiah. Each antiphon calls out to the Lord under a different title. The "O" antiphons are sung in the verses of the Advent song "O Come, O Come, Emmanuel." Have the students illustrate the antiphons in white ovals for display using the symbols in italics on the chart.

"O" Antiphons

| December 17: | O Wisdom, O holy Word of God, you govern all creation with your strong yet tender care. |
| *triangle* | Come and show your people the way to salvation. |

| December 18: | O Sacred Lord of ancient Israel, you showed yourself to Moses in the burning bush, and gave him the holy law on Sinai mountain. |
| *tablets* | Come, stretch out your mighty hand to set us free. |

| December 19: | O flower of Jesse's stem, you have been raised up as a sign for all people; kings stand silent in your presence; nations bow down in worship before you. |
| *flower* | Come, let nothing keep you from coming to our aid. |

| December 20: | O Key of David, O royal Power of Israel. You control at will the gate of heaven. |
| *key* | Come, break down the prison walls of death for those who dwell in darkness and the shadow of death; lead your captive people into freedom. |

| December 21: | O Radiant Dawn, you are the splendor of eternal light, the sun of justice. |
| *sunrise* | Come, shine on those who dwell in darkness and the shadow of death. |

| December 22: | O King of all nations, you are the only joy of every heart, the Keystone of the mighty arch of humankind. |
| *crown* | Come, and save the creature you fashioned from dust. |

| December 23: | O Emmanuel, you are King and Lawgiver, desire of the nations, Savior of all people. |
| *manger* | Come, and set us free, Lord our God. |

Christmas

• *Christmas carols* • Analyze Christmas carols for the theology contained in them and then sing them.

• *Poem-prayer* • Have the students write a poem-prayer to Jesus about his coming at Christmas.

• *La Posada* • Celebrate the Hispanic custom of La Posada. Two students represent Mary and Joseph seeking lodging for the night. Luminarias light the way. These are paper bags weighted with sand and with a candle inside. The tops of the bags can be turned down two inches for more stability. The couple is turned away from door after door. When they are finally welcomed, the students celebrate, perhaps by breaking open a piñata.

• *Tree blessing* • Send home a Christmas tree blessing for families to use, or bless a tree and nativity set in the school.

• *Epiphany* • Hold an Epiphany prayer service in which the students present the Child Jesus with spiritual gifts written on paper or monetary gifts for the missions.

Lent
• *Stations* • Pray the Stations of the Cross with the students. See "Way of the Cross" on page 63.

• *Prayer to Jesus* • Have the students write a prayer to Jesus on the cross.

• *Pretzels and prayer* • Introduce Lent as a time of prayer by distributing pretzels. Explain that originally pretzels represented arms folded in prayer. Encourage the students to schedule a special time of prayer in their day during Lent.

• *Easter triduum* • Strongly suggest that the students participate in the Easter triduum services with their families.

• *Illustrated one-line prayers* • Have the students write short one-line prayers concerning the suffering and death of Jesus and illustrate them.

• *Seder meal* • Celebrate a Christian seder meal.

Easter
• *Hymns* • Sing Easter hymns and discuss their lyrics.

• *Prayers* • Have the students write prayers to the Risen Lord.

• *Alleluia* • Tell the students the meaning of *Alleluia*, the Easter word. (*Hallel* is Hebrew for "praise," and *Yah* is the first syllable of Yahweh. *Alleluia* means "Praise the Lord.") Teach a sung Alleluia.

• *Exultet/Sequence* • Use missalettes to introduce the students to the Exultet sung at the Saturday night Easter Vigil services and the Sequence for Easter Sunday.

• *Psalm* • Have the students write an Easter psalm.

Pentecost
• *Prayer to the Holy Spirit* • Teach the students the prayer to the Holy Spirit. Encourage them to pray it before reading Scripture and before making an important decision.

• *The Sequence* • Present the Pentecost Sequence and ask the students what they learn about the Holy Spirit from it.

• *Seven gifts* • Have the students write a prayer to the Holy Spirit for each of the seven gifts. Display these prayers in flames of fire on the bulletin board or wall, or in a mobile.

Church Unity Octave

• *Church unity octave prayers* • Tell the history of this observance on which we pray for the unity of all Christians. Pray the church unity octave prayers in class from January 18 to January 25, or have the students pray them at home.

• *A visitor* • Arrange a class visit to a church of another faith tradition or invite another class to your church. Give a tour and then hold a prayer service for the intention of church unity.

• *Guest speakers* • Have a person or a panel of people from other faith traditions speak to your class about their religious services. Pray with them.

First Friday Novenas in Honor of the Sacred Heart

• *Meaning of the Sacred Heart* • Discuss the significance of the heart as a symbol of love and as a symbol of the whole person of Jesus. Discuss the significance of the Sacred Heart of Jesus as a heart that has loved us to the point of suffering and dying for us. This devotion centers on the humanity of Jesus.

• *The story* • Tell about St. Margaret Mary Alacoque and St. Claude de la Colombière and the twelve promises Jesus made to St. Margaret Mary in her private revelations.

• *A visual* • Show a picture or statue of the Sacred Heart. Explain that the heart of Christ revealed to Margaret Mary was crowned with thorns, pierced, and surmounted by the cross. It was a heart on fire with love.

• *First Fridays* • Explain the practice of receiving Holy Communion in honor of the Sacred Heart on the first Friday of nine consecutive months.

• *Litany* • Pray the litany of the Sacred Heart with your students.

Purposes
of Prayer

I ask that supplications, prayers, petitions, and thanksgivings be offered for everyone.

1 Timothy 2:1

How good it is to hear someone praying for you. Once I had the privilege of living for two months at the Shelter of God's Love in Chicago during the final stages of a religion series I was working on. An intercessory community lives there: eight people with disabilities and Rosemary Koenig, the founder, who is a spunky Irish woman. Every night after supper, the community prays together for various intentions. To hear these people pray for me by name, spelling out my needs, gave me strength and courage—and helped finish the series on time.

Although petition is probably the most common type of prayer, we also pray to adore God and express our love, to ask forgiveness, and to thank God.

• *Acronyms for reasons to pray* • Discuss reasons for prayer. You can use the traditional acronym ACTS for adoration, contrition, thanksgiving, and supplication, but I prefer PACT (petition, adoration, contrition, and thanksgiving.) *Petition* is easier to remember than *supplication*, and the word *pact* is a reminder that prayer is related to a love relationship, a covenant.

    Petition: We ask for our needs.
    Adoration: We worship God and acknowledge God's greatness.
    Contrition: We express sorrow for our sins and failings and ask forgiveness.
    Thanksgiving: We show appreciation and gratitude for God's gifts.

• *Psalms* • Present the purposes for prayer through psalms. Have the students read psalms like the following and tell what each psalm expresses (adoration, contrition, thanksgiving, or petition). Then have them find other psalms or verses that do the same.

    Psalm 19 (adoration)
    Psalm 51 (contrition)
    Psalm 69 (petition)
    Psalm 75 (thanksgiving)

• *Mass prayers* • Have the students use missalettes to find examples of each type of prayer in the Mass.

• *Benefits of prayer* • Point out the benefits of prayer. Begin by asking the students why they pray.

• *Prayers as gifts* • Explain that we can give one another the gift of prayers. We used to do this in the form of a Spiritual Bouquet, a list of prayers and how many of each we promised to pray for a person. Students can include prayers as a gift to a loved one or to someone who is sick.

• *Prayers made public* • Post a large sheet of poster paper or a strip of shelf paper on the wall for the students to add original prayers to from time to time. Or make a large booklet of blank pages for the students' prayers and keep it on a table or in the prayer corner.

Prayer Requests and Intentions

A little boy knelt by his bed and prayed, "Dear God, please take care of Mommy and Daddy, and my little sister, and Grandma, and please God, take care of yourself, because if anything happens to you, we're all sunk." Because of our dependence on God and our trust in his love, we turn to him in confidence in all our needs. Those who are inclined to regard petition as a second-class prayer should recall that the Our Father, the perfect prayer, contains seven petitions.

• *Class sessions offered for students* • Offer each class session for a particular student. Pass around a calendar and let the students sign up for a day they would like the class to pray for them. They usually choose their birthday or the day of a big test.

• *Praying for a classmate* • Put all of the students' names in a box. Pass around the box and have the students each draw a name for a classmate to pray for in a special way during the year or during a month.

• *Expressed intentions* • Let the students offer intentions at the beginning of each class. An added advantage of this is that it helps you know your students and where they're coming from.

• *General intentions for Mass* • Arrange opportunities for your class to compose the general intercessions for Mass.

• *A prayer corner for intentions* • Designate a part of a blackboard or bulletin board as the Prayer Corner on which students post special needs that require prayer. On the bulletin board put pockets for intentions labeled "Church," "World," "Others' Needs," and "Our Needs." Or keep a list of intentions on the board.

• *Newspaper clippings* • Make a bulletin board on which the students post newspaper clippings of people and situations that need prayer.

• *Current needs* • Mention current needs yourself in your class prayers.

• *Prayer basket* • Have a prayer basket in the room into which students place prayer requests. These may be read at the beginning of class, or the basket may be passed around and students may draw out a request to pray for during the week.

• *Imaged answers to requests* • Encourage the students to image the answer to their prayers as they pray. For instance, during prayer for the recovery of a sick person, they visualize the person in the peak of health, going about normal activities.

• *Prayer pen pals* • Organize prayer pen pals for your class. Pair your students with parishioners, students in another class, or senior citizens in an assisted living residence or nursing home. Throughout the year on special occasions or in a special time of need, have the students write to their partners with a promise of prayer and a request for their partner's prayers.

• *Praying for enemies* • Point out that the strongest way to change an enemy into a friend is to pray for that person, perhaps because prayer changes our own attitudes. Quote Jesus' teaching about this: "But I say to you, love your enemies, and pray for those who persecute you" (Matthew 5:44).

• *Prayer stories* • Share stories with the students about prayers that have been answered. For instance, tell the story of Eddie Rickenbacker and seven others who crashed into the Pacific Ocean during World War II. All they had to eat was four oranges. The men prayed together every day. After a week it rained, and they had water to drink. One day a seagull landed on Rickenbacker's head. He caught it and the men had food. When rescue came after twenty-one days, all but one of the eight men had survived.

• *Vigil lights* • Explain the custom of lighting vigil lights as a sign of our prayer rising up to God. We make a donation, light a candle, and pray for a certain intention, usually that a deceased person may have eternal life. Decide on a class intention and then take your students to church, make a donation, light a vigil light, and pray together.

Qualities
of a Good Pray-er

If you have faith the size of a mustard seed, you would say to [this] mulberry tree, "Be up-rooted and planted in the sea," and it would obey you.   Luke 17:6

Teach the qualities of a good pray-er: availability, honesty, trust, and perseverance. Persons of prayer are open to God and to the wonders of the world that convey God's messages. They spend time communicating with God and pondering God's goodness and love. Persons of prayer are honest before God. They are themselves and express their true feelings. Persons of prayer trust God. They believe in God's promises and have faith in God's loving plan for them. And persons of prayer never endanger their relationship with God by impeding or stopping communication. Even when it is difficult, they patiently, relentlessly seek to be aware of God's presence and love.

• *Jesus and the saints as pray-ers* • Have the students reflect on the prayer of people who are known for being good pray-ers (Jesus, Mary, and the saints) and find the qualities of a good pray-er in them.

Availability

• *Waiting for the Lord* • Prayerful persons plan spaces in their days for God. Tell the students that the American author Flannery O'Connor described waiting for inspiration in a way that also describes waiting for the Lord to speak. She said:

> "Every morning between 9 and 12, I go to my room and sit before a piece of paper. Many times I just sit for three hours with no ideas coming to me. But I know one thing: If an idea does come between 9 and 12, I am there ready for it."

• *Making time* • Explain to your students that it is important to make time for prayer. Use the example of a child who longs to be friends with his older brother, but the brother never has time to talk to the child. The two barely know each other even though they live together. If our minds are always racing with ideas and plans, if we are always occupied with other things so that we never give God an opportunity to speak, how will we ever develop a relationship with God? We will be strangers when we meet face to face!

• *Jesus knocking* • Show or tell about the famous picture of Jesus knocking on the door. Ask what is unusual about the door. (It has no handle or doorknob.) Ask the students what this means. Remind them that Jesus said, "Behold, I stand at the door and knock" (Revelation 3:20). He won't break the door down. If we don't open it, Jesus won't enter.

Honesty

• *Dropping our masks* • God knows us through and through, as Psalm 139 reminds us. It is useless and foolish to pose before God as something we are not. Point out to the students that when conversing with God, it is all right to be angry. It is also all right to laugh. There is no need to hide our fears from God or our faults. Explain that God is a friend with whom we can drop our masks and enjoy the freedom of being completely ourselves.

• *True prayers* • Read the students this advice from Hasidic tradition, the mystics of Judaism:

> Do not think that the words of prayers as you say them go up to God. It is not the words themselves that ascend; rather it is the burning desire of your heart that rises like smoke to heaven. If your prayer consists only of words and letters, but does not contain your heart's desire, how can it rise up to God?

Trust

Faith is intimately bound to prayer. If we believe God and trust in his love for us, we will pray with confidence.

• *Miracles of faith* • Recall for the students that Jesus' miracles were often worked in response to a person's faith. Refer to the centurion in Luke 7:1-10, Jairus in Luke 8:49-56, and the blind beggar in Luke 18:35-43.

• *Past blessings* • Have the students list all the things that God has already provided for them. Then tell them to list their prayers that God has already answered. Invite them to reflect on the Father's love for them in the past as an encouragement to trust God now.

• *Assuring scriptural passages* • Present to the students scriptural passages that highlight the extraordinary love God has for us, such as the following:

> I will never forget you.
> See, upon the palms of my hands
> I have written your name.
> Isaiah 49:15-16

• *Working along with praying* • Warn the students not to use prayer as a substitute for their own efforts. Tell them the adage, "Pray as though it all depended on God; work as though it all depended on you."

Perseverance

Praying isn't easy. Even the great Teresa of Avila sometimes experienced problems. She admitted shaking the hourglass during prayer to speed up the time.

• *Two parables about perseverance* • Remind the students of Jesus' two parables that teach us to pray with persistence: the widow who hounds the judge until he gives in and the friend who comes in the middle of the night for bread and doesn't give up until he gets it. Have them act out these parables to reinforce their message.

• *Stories of perseverance* • Tell the students stories about people who prayed for a long time and eventually received what they asked for. St. Monica and her prayers for her wayward son Augustine are one example. You probably can relate your own personal stories.

Resources
for Prayer

At that very moment he rejoiced [in] the holy Spirit and said, "I give you praise, Father, Lord of heaven and earth, for although you have hidden these things from the wise and the learned you have revealed them to the childlike." 　　　　　　　　　　　　Luke 10:21

A torrent of materials on prayer is flooding the market today, a sign of people's awakened interest in spirituality. Following is an annotated bibliography for teachers and students.

Books for catechists

Barr, Robert R. *Scriptural Comfort for Trying Times*. Huntington, Ind.: Our Sunday Visitor, 1992. Reflections on scriptural passages that correspond to 52 difficult times we might experience.

Barry, William J. *God and You*. Mahwah, N.J.: Paulist Press, 1987.

Bergan, Jacqueline Syrup, and Marie Schwan. Take and Receive series. *Birth, Forgiveness, Freedom, Love, Surrender*. Winona, Minn.: St. Mary's Press, 1985, 1985, 1988, 1985, 1986. Daily meditations beginning with a scriptural passage. Includes a commentary and a suggestion for prayer.

Bloom, Anthony. *Beginning to Pray*. New York: Paulist Press, 1970. A classic primer on prayer.

Brook, John. *The School of Prayer: An Introduction to the Divine Office for All Christians*. Collegeville, Minn.: The Liturgical Press, 1991. The principles and practice of praying morning, evening, and night prayer.

Costello, Gwen. *Prayer Services for Religious Educators*. Mystic, Conn.: Twenty-Third Publications, 1989. 32 short prayer experiences for groups involved in faith sharing on topics such as justice, peace, service, and being open to God's will.

Cunningham, Lawrence S. *Catholic Prayer*. New York: Crossroad, 1989. An excellent overview of prayer in the Catholic tradition, considering the pray-er, words, gestures, reading, Jesus, the Eucharist, models, politics, and stages.

Davidson, Graeme J., with Mary McDonald. *Anyone Can Pray: A Guide to Methods of Christian Prayer*. New York: Paulist Press, 1983. A handbook on different ways to pray.

Deiss, Lucien, C.S.Sp. *Come Lord Jesus: Biblical Prayers with Psalms and Scripture Readings*. Chicago: World Library Publications, 1981.

de Mello, Anthony, S.J. *Flight of the Bird*. New York: Doubleday, 1990. Stories for reflection.

_____. *One Minute Wisdom*. New York: Doubleday, 1988. Stories for reflection.

_____. *Sadhana: A Way to God*. New York: Doubleday, 1984. A simple presentation of advice on praying and many exercises on meditation and contemplation drawn from the church's tradition, St. Ignatius's *Spiritual Exercises*, and oriental techniques.

_____. *Song of the Bird*. New York: Doubleday, 1984. Stories for reflection.

Edwards, Tilden. *Living Simply through the Day*. Mahwah, N.J.: Paulist Press, 1977.

Farrell, Edward. *Prayer Is a Hunger*. Denville, N. J.: Dimension Books, 1972.

Finley, James. *The Awakening Call: Fostering Intimacy with God*. Notre Dame, Ind.: Ave Maria Press, 1985. A guide to contemplative prayer that relates Christian traditions to our lives today.

Fiorenza, Joseph A. *Sunday, the Original Feast Day*. Collegeville, Minn.: The Liturgical Press, 1989. The importance of celebrating Sunday.

Gallagher, Maureen, Clare Wagner, and David Woeste. *Praying with Scripture*. Mahwah, N.J.: Paulist Press, 1983.

Glavich, Mary Kathleen, S.N.D. *Voices: Messages in Gospel Symbols*. Mystic, Conn.: Twenty-Third Publications, 1987. Reflections on 15 symbols in the Gospels.

Greene, Thomas, S.J. *Opening to God: A Guide to Prayer*. Notre Dame, Ind.: Ave Maria Press, 1977. An introduction to prayer.

_____. *When the Well Runs Dry: Prayer beyond the Beginnings*. Notre Dame, Ind.: Ave Maria Press, 1979.

Groeschel, Benedict J., C.F.R. *Listening at Prayer*. New York: Paulist Press, 1983. A guide to listening to God, the key to encountering God in a fresh way.

Hall, Thelma, P.C. *Too Deep for Words: Rediscovering Lectio Divina*. New York: Paulist Press, 1988. Describes the history and process of this method and offers 500 scriptural passages for prayer.

Hays, Edward. *Prayers for a Planetary Pilgrim: A Personal Manual for Prayer and Ritual*. Easton, Kans.: Forest of Peace Books, 1989. Creative prayers.

Hutchinson, Gloria. *Praying the Rosary: New Reflections on the Mysteries*. Cincinnati: St. Anthony Messenger Press, 1991. Reflections that help make the mysteries relevant to people today. Also suitable for high school students.

_____. *Six Ways to Pray from Six Great Saints*. Cincinnati: St. Anthony Messenger Press, 1982. Approaches to prayer from Francis, Clare, Ignatius, Thérèse, Teresa, and John.

Kirvan, John, and Roger Radley (eds.). *Our Heritage Is the Lord: A Book of Prayer*. Minneapolis: Winston Press Inc., 1980.

Labat, Elizabeth-Paule, O.S.B. *The Presence of God*. Trans. by David Smith. Mahwah, N.J.: Paulist Press, 1979.

Link, Mark, S.J. *You: Prayer for Beginners and Those Who Have Forgotten How*. Niles,

Ill.: Argus Communications, 1976. An interesting how-to-pray program that covers the essentials of prayer.

Main, John. *Moment of Christ: The Path of Meditation*. New York: Crossroad. 1984. A guide to meditation by simply repeating a mantra.

Maloney, George A., S.J. *Journey into Contemplation*. Locust Valley, N.Y.: Living Flame Press, 1983. A guide for contemplative prayer.

Meehan, Bridget, S.S.C. *Nine Ways to Reach God: A Prayer Sampler*. Liguori, Mo.: Liguori Publications, 1990. Explores nine ways of praying for individuals and groups.

Moran, Pamela (ed.). *A Marian Prayer Book: A Treasury of Prayers, Hymns, and Meditations*. Ann Arbor, Mich.: Servant Publications, 1991. A collection of traditional and contemporary prayers. Includes reflections by spiritual writers, saints, and theologians.

Muto, Susan Annette. *Meditation in Motion*. New York: Doubleday, 1986. Explains in an interesting way how everyone can pray during and about everyday events. Each chapter begins and ends with a meditation exercise.

Nouwen, Henri J. M. *With Open Hands*. Notre Dame, Ind.: Ave Maria Press, 1972. Shows how moments of prayer occur in everyday life; eloquent photographs.

Pennington, Basil, O.C.S.O. *Challenges in Prayer*. Wilmington: Michael Glazier, Inc., 1982. An introduction to prayer, including contemplative prayer.

_____. *Centering Prayer*. Garden City, New York: Doubleday, Image Books, 1980. The practice of centering prayer.

Pennock, Michael Francis. *The Ways of Prayer: An Introduction*. Notre Dame, Ind.: Ave Maria Press, 1987. A practical book on prayer with discussions of traditional methods.

Rinker, Rosalind. *Learning Conversational Prayer*. Collegeville, Minn.: The Liturgical Press, 1992. A simple explanation of an effective way to pray aloud with others.

Books for families

Bishops' Committee on the Liturgy, National Conference of Catholic Bishops. *Catholic Household Blessings & Prayers*. Washington, D.C.: U.S. Catholic Conference, 1988. A collection of prayers for every family occasion.

DeGidio, Sandra, O.S.M. *Enriching Faith through Family Celebrations*. Mystic, Conn.: Twenty-Third Publications, 1989.

Goodwin, Lawrence J. *Christian Family Celebrations: Prayer Services for Special Moments*. Mahwah, N.J.: Paulist Press. Simple, meaningful rituals that enhance moments related to the church year.

Hays, Edward. *Prayers for the Domestic Church*. Easton, Kans.: Forest of Peace Books, 1989. A variety of prayers that can be used in the home and other places.

Travnikar, Rock, O.F.M. *The Blessing Cup: 24 Symbolic Rites for Family Prayer Celebrations*. Cincinnati: St. Anthony Messenger Press, 1979. Short celebrations that include the sharing of a common cup.

Books for catechesis

Atwood, Corey. *Banners for Beginners*. Wilton, Conn.: Morehouse, Barlow, 1987.

Bannon, J.F., et. al. *Prayer Forms: 22 Prayer Forms for Classrooms & Youth Groups*. Mystic, Conn.: Twenty-Third Publications, 1985. Plans for carrying out a variety of prayer experiences collected by the Christian Brothers.

Black, Barbara, Karen Jessie, and John Paulett. *Pentecost, Peanuts, Popcorn, Prayer*. Villa Maria, Penn.: The Center for Learning, 1988. 42 communal prayer experiences for teenagers and young adults.

Brokamp, Marilyn, O.S.F. *Prayer Times for Intermediate Grades*. Cincinnati: St. Anthony Messenger Press, 1987. Presents a variety of prayer styles in 27 brief services rooted in the world of the schoolchild.

_____. *Prayer Times for Primary Grades*. Cincinnati: St. Anthony Messenger Press, 1987.

Caprio, Betsy. *Experiments in Prayer*. Notre Dame, Ind.: Ave Maria Press, 1973. Offers many creative ideas for prayer.

Costello, Gwen. *Praying with Children: 28 Prayer Services for Various Occasions*. Mystic, Conn.: Twenty-Third Publications, 1990. Covers the seasons of the year, liturgical seasons and feasts, and happenings in the lives of children.

Cronin, Gaynell. *Sunday throughout the Week*. Notre Dame, Ind.: Ave Maria Press, 1981.

Darcy-Berube, Francoise, and John Paul Berube. *Someone's There: Paths to Prayer for Young People*. Notre Dame, Ind.: Ave Maria Press, 1987.

Dollen, Charles (ed.). *Prayer Book of the Saints*. Huntington, Ind.: Our Sunday Visitor, 1984. A collection of saints' prayers from the church's beginnings to modern times.

Donze, Mary Terese, A.S.C. *Prayer and Our Children: Passing on the Tradition*. Notre Dame, Ind.: Ave Maria Press, 1987.

_____. *In My Heart Room: 16 Love Prayers for Little Children*. Liguori, Mo.: Liguori Publications, 1982. Meditations for children six to ten years old with this format: concentrating on an object, meditating on the object, and then contemplating, or resting in God's presence.

_____. *In My Heart Room, Book Two: More Love Prayers for Children*. Liguori, Mo.: Liguori Publications, 1990.

Dues, Greg. *Seasonal Prayer Services for Teenagers*. Mystic, Conn.: Twenty-Third Publications, 1991. Stimulating prayer activities that appeal to teenagers.

Grgic, Bob. *Journey to the Father*. Dubuque: Brown Publishing-ROA Media, 1987. Prayer for high school students.

Halpin, Marlene, O.P. *Imagine That!* Dubuque: Wm. C. Brown Co., 1981. 15 fantasies for prayer.

_____. *Puddles of Knowing: Engaging Children in Our Prayer Heritage,* Dubuque: Wm. C. Brown Co., 1984. Ideas for prayer from the author's experience of conducting a prayer center in a school.

Hamma, Robert. *Still More Children's Liturgies.* Mahwah, N.J.: Paulist Press. 134 celebrations for children of all ages.

Hesch, John B. *Prayer & Meditation for Middle School Kids.* Mahwah, N.J.: Paulist Press, 1985. Step-by-step meditations.

Hilliard, Dick, and Beverly Valenti-Hilliard. *Come and Celebrate: More Center Celebrations.* Notre Dame, Ind.: Ave Maria Press, 1985. 26 liturgical events for children from grades K to 5.

Jeep, Elizabeth McMahon. *Children's Daily Prayer.* Chicago: Liturgy Training Publications, 1991. A rich collection of prayers for school use: morning, lunchtime, and end of the day, based on prayers in the Liturgy of the Hours.

Jessie, Karen. *Praying with Children,* Book 1 (Grades 1-3); Book 2 (Grades 4-6). Villa Maria, Penn.: The Center for Learning, 1991. Each book contains 20 prayer services.

Machado, Mary Kathryn. *How to Plan Children's Liturgies.* San Jose, Cal.: Resource Publications, 1985.

Mathson, Patricia. *Pray & Play: 28 Prayer Services and Activities for Children in K through Sixth Grade.* Notre Dame, Ind.: Ave Maria Press, 1989. Short prayer services that include a biblical reading followed by one or two enrichment activities.

Manternach, Janaan, with Carl J. Pfeifer. *And the Children Pray.* Notre Dame, Ind.: Ave Maria Press, 1989. A guide to what prayer is, attitudes and conditions that support prayer, and ways that teachers can help themselves and children learn to pray. Incorporates many personal stories and examples.

Nestojko, Jeanne, and Jean Pieper. *More Pocket Prayers for Young Christians.* Los Angeles: Franciscan Communications, 1990. Small booklet of relevant prayers for youth.

Pastva, Loretta, S.N.D. *Seeking God, Learning to Love, Transformations, Contemplation.* Encino, Cal.: Benziger, 1979. Books filled with creative ideas for a high school course on prayer.

Puig, Enric. *Lord, I Am One of Your Little Ones: Prayers for Children.* Chicago: Loyola University Press, 1987. Prayers for children from six to ten composed by other children.

Reehorst, Jane, B.V.M. *Guided Meditations for Children: How to Teach Children to Pray Using Scripture,* Vol. 1 (intermediate), 2 (primary), 3 (high school). Dubuque: Wm. C. Brown, 1986, 1991, 1992. Using their five senses in line with the Ignatian form of meditation, children set a scriptural scene that serves as a backdrop for meeting the Lord.

Rezy, Carol. *Liturgies for Little Ones: 38 Celebrations for Grades One to Three*. Notre Dame, Ind.: Ave Maria Press, 1978. Offers liturgies with themes dealing with the life of Jesus as well as family, sharing, forgiveness, seasons, and feasts.

Roslak, Deborah, and Linda Joy Orber. *Dear Jesus ... Dear Child: Guided Meditations for Young Children*. Mystic, Conn.: Twenty-Third Publications, 1992. Leads children to pray through letters to and from Jesus about children's concerns.

Sacred Heart League. *Tracks: A Young Way to God*. Walls, Miss.: Sacred Heart League, 1985. A prayerbook for pre-teens and teens with prayers composed by Sacred Heart Fathers and Brothers and young people.

Scheihing, Theresa O'Callahan, with Louis M. Savary. *Our Treasured Heritage: Teaching Christian Meditation to Children*. New York: Crossroad, 1981. Suggestions for centering and meditating with children for teachers and parents. Includes seven meditations for the liturgical year based on the Ignatian form.

Audiotapes and records
Suppliers of religious music:

Credence Cassettes
115 E. Armour Blvd.
P.O. Box 419491
Kansas City, MO 64141-6491

Maranatha! Music
P.O. Box 1396
Costa Mesa, CA 92626

GIA Publications, Inc.
7404 South Mason Avenue
Chicago, IL 60638

North American Liturgy Resources (NALR)
10802 N. 23rd Avenue
Phoenix, AZ 85029

Videotapes
Celebrating the Church Year for Children. Gaynell Cronin and Jack Rathschmidt, O.F.M. Cap. Paulist Press. 6 videos that present the meaning of and customs for the celebration of the seasons of the year, Christmas and Easter, and Mary.

Learning the Art of Prayer. Benedict Groeschel, C.F.R. Paulist Press. 7 cassettes on various prayer techniques.

Let Us Pray...for Young Children. Gaynell Cronin. Iconographics. Different ways that children from ages 6-10 can pray.

Our Christian Prayers. ROA Media. Develops attitudes and practices of prayer in children from grades 4 through 12.

Prayer. ROA Media. Prayer from six different perspectives for grade 7 and up.

Prayer Celebrates God's Love. ROA Media. Helps children in grades K-3 learn to pray like Jesus.

Prayer in Your Home. Franciscan Communications. The possibilities of prayer within five symbolic home activities.

The Psalm series. Treehaus Communications. 5 videos on the themes of hope, joy, peace, love, and thanksgiving; each has 3-5 minute reflections on particular psalms.

The Seven Circles of Prayer. Franciscan Communications. Inspiring photography, drama, and commentary help the viewer meet God in prayer.

Traditional Prayers for Children. Paulist Press. Explores the Our Father, Hail Mary, Apostles Creed, and Glory Be with scriptural images and modern day pictures for children ages 6 to 9.

Wake Up! Spirituality for Today. Anthony de Mello, S.J. Tabor Publishing. Praying from the heart.

Periodicals

Catechist
2451 East River Road
Dayton, OH 45439
A magazine with many ideas for catechists.

Living Prayer
Beckley Hill,
Barre, VT 05641
A bimonthly publication of articles on prayer.

Modern Liturgy
160 E. Virginia St. #290
San Jose, CA 95112
A magazine with ideas for celebrating liturgy.

Praying
115 E. Armour Blvd.
P.O. Box 410335
Kansas City, MO 64141
A bimonthly journal with stories, articles, and reflections on prayer.

Religion Teacher's Journal
P.O. Box 180
Mystic, CT 06355
A magazine for catechists, with an annual issue on prayer.

Share the Word
Paulist National Catholic Evangelization Association
3031 Fourth Street, N.E.
Washington, D.C. 20017
A bimonthly booklet with excellent background on each Sunday's readings and a prayer service. Good for individuals and groups. Available free.

Posters
Argus Posters
P.O. Box 7000
Allen, TX 75002
1-800-527-4748

Concordia Publishing House
3558 South Jefferson Avenue
St. Louis, MO 63118
1-800-325-3040

Daughters of St. Paul
50 St. Paul's Avenue
Boston, MA 02130
1-800-876-4463

David C. Cook Publishing House
850 North Grove Avenue
Elgin, IL 60120
1-800-323-7543

Don Bosco Multimedia
475 North Avenue, Box T
New Rochelle, NY 10802
1-800-342-5850

Loyola University Press
3441 North Ashland Avenue
Chicago, IL 60657
1-800-621-1008

Slides
Center for Learning
P.O. Box 910
Villa Maria, PA 16155
Images of Life Slide Prayer Packages: 300 slides, books, tapes
1-800-767-9090

Silence
and Stillness

Be still, and know that I am God. Psalm 46:10 (RSV)

All of us have experiences stashed away in our memories that bear out the truth of the saying "silence is golden." Maybe you remember walking into the peace of your own home after a noisy party, or taking a stroll before anyone else was awake, or gazing at a baby fast asleep.

Such times are valuable because they draw us more deeply into reality. Usually the world packs our minds with a million noises: music, chatter, commercials, traffic sounds, crowds. Sheltered from these distractions, we are free to concentrate on essentials. In silence we find truth, goodness, and beauty. In silence we discover who we are. Silence is the air that our spirit must breathe if our spiritual life is to thrive.

What is vitally important is that when we sink into silence, we come face to face with God. To be still, we must cease our frantic pace, quiet our bodies, curb our racing minds, and close our mouths. Only when we are still can we be attuned to the voice of God speaking from the eternal silence. This is the message of Elijah's encounter with Yahweh. Elijah journeys to the mountain of God and there God is revealed, not in a mighty wind, not in an earthquake, not in fire but in the sound of a gentle breeze.

Jesus, our exemplar for sound living, valued silence. He prepared for his public life by a 40-day private retreat in the wilderness. Before choosing his apostles, "He departed to the mountain to pray, and he spent the night in prayer to God" (Luke 6:12). He often got up before dawn or drew apart from the crowds to commune with God alone, to celebrate their bond of love, and to center his life and his work on God's will. Jesus recommended prayer in solitude to his followers: "But when you pray, go to your inner room, close the door, and pray to your Father in secret " (Matthew 6:6).

We believe that the Trinity lives within us. Quiet solitude enables us to attend to the divine presence. We can adore God in the depth of our being, delight in God's loving presence, and strengthen our love for God. As a prayer card rightly states, "Silence is the profound activity of listening love." Refreshed and encouraged by loving encounters with our God, we can better meet the challenges of life.

People seeking God have always reserved silent spaces in their lives. Thomas More, for instance, who was Chancellor of England in the sixteenth century, prayed every morning from two to six o'clock. For centuries men and women religious have practiced silence. Serious Christians participate in days of recollection, retreats, and renewals in which silence plays a major role. Even during liturgical celebrations "at the proper times all should observe a reverent silence." The *Directory for Masses with Children* asks us to instill in children human values that provide a foundation for the celebration of the Eucharist. It recommends teaching students to appreciate silence and to use it to enter within themselves.

The following ideas help your students to have truly pregnant silence. In the Christmas liturgy we hear "When peaceful silence lay over all, and night had run the half of her swift course, down from the heavens, from the royal throne, leapt your all-powerful Word" (Wisdom 18:14-15). Our silent hearts invite another incarnation. In the tranquility of silence the Word becomes living and active in us. Faith, hope, and love are born anew. We acquire the energy to live life to the hilt, and we increase our potential for eternal life. As God's spokespersons, we are responsible for sharing the secret of the power of silence with those we teach.

• *A self-check* • Give the students a self-check like the following one to see how they value silence. Take it yourself.

1. Am I afraid to be alone?
2. Am I uncomfortable doing nothing?
3. Do I occasionally treat myself to several hours of solitude and silence—in a park, at the beach, or some other secluded area?
4. During how much of each day do I actually experience silence?
5. Do I always have the radio on when I drive?
6. In the quiet evening hours do I always watch TV, or do I sometimes pray, read, or reflect?
7. After receiving communion, do I pray—or watch people go by?
8. How much time do I allow for daily prayer?

• *The need for silence* • Stress the need for silence. Jesus said, "Behold I stand at the door and knock." Let the students know that he doesn't pound. He knocks. They won't hear him knocking if they always have their Walkman over their ears.

• *An opening prayer* • Pray this prayer to begin class (or for periods of reflection or to introduce prayer services): Jesus, you speak to me when I am silent. Once amid thunder and crashing waves when you said, "Peace, be still," the wind and the waves obeyed you. Now calm me, Lord. Quiet my body so that I might rest in your presence. Silence my heart and mind so that I might wait attentively for your word. Then when I am still, speak, Lord, and I will listen.

• *Modeling silence* • Model silence for your students. When they are being reflective, be reflective with them instead of looking over lesson plans, flipping pages, or preparing materials. Move quietly; answer questions gently.

• *Listening to silence* • Invite your students to "listen" to silence for a few minutes during each class. Ask them to describe what it sounds like and what they were aware of as they listened. (With luck, no one's stomach will growl.)

• *Listening bodies* • Begin class for younger children by inviting them to have listening hands, listening feet, and listening eyes. To really listen, these body parts must be still and quiet. When necessary, during the course of the lesson repeat this invitation to remind the children of the value of silence.

• *The still of a pond* • Use the analogy of a pond when teaching stillness. A pond that is disturbed and full of ripples reflects a distorted view of the world, while a still pond reflects the world clearly. We must be still for a clear view of life.

• *Settling activities* • Learn and use settling activities with little children. For example, have the children sit on the floor and chant three times "I'm quiet as a bug in a rug." Each time they should soften their voices so that the third time the sentence is only whispered.

• *Discussion* • Discuss silence by asking questions like the following:

1. What good things happen in silence? (The sun sets and rises, flowers grow, snow falls, stars shine, and cookies bake. You can see deer, catch fish, read a book, and work out a problem.)
2. What are some places where people keep silent—and why? (People keep silent in a library in order to concentrate, in a hospital so patients can rest and be healed, in a museum to better appreciate the masterpieces, in a cemetery out of respect for the dead, and in church to show reverence for God.)
3. Why do we need silence? (We need silence to think, to see things in a new perspective, to be at peace, to reflect on our lives, to be renewed, to reenter the world within us, and to make contact with God.)
4. What role did silence play in Jesus' life? (Jesus was born in the still of the night. He prayed alone before his public life began, before choosing his apostles, and before the crucifixion. He often withdrew to pray alone in silence during the night and early in the morning.)

Times
of Prayer

So God blessed the seventh day and made it holy, because on it he rested from all the work he had done in creation.   Genesis 2:3

As a means to develop spiritual life, individuals are encouraged to mark off definite times for prayer. These include certain times during each day for private prayer, triduums and novenas for special occasions, as well as longer periods like days of recollection and retreats. In addition, all faith traditions set aside special time during which all members devote themselves to prayer. In the Judaic-Christian tradition, one day a week is considered sacred time—the Sabbath. To extend the celebration of significant feasts, Christians observe vigils and octaves. The following activities prepare students to appreciate and adopt the practice of observing holy times.

• *A time and place* • Allow time in class for students to decide a time and place for prayer if they are not already accustomed to daily prayer. Have them make their decision in the context of a meditation. Invite them to imagine that Jesus is with them viewing the possible places and times they could pray. Suggest that they ask him to help them choose the best time to meet with him every day.

• *Prayer services* • Celebrate feast days with a special prayer service that the students plan and participate in.

• *Days of recollection and retreats* • Hold a day of recollection for the class or a weekend retreat. Call it Bethany day (in memory of the time Jesus spent with his friends Lazarus, Mary, and Martha in Bethany) or Tabor days (in memory of the day Jesus revealed his glory on Mount Tabor to Peter, James, and John). Plan activities that will strengthen the students' relationship with God:

> communal prayer
> personal prayer
> talks for reflection
> a film or video to stimulate thought
> inspirational readings available
> the Eucharist
> the possibility of receiving the sacrament of reconciliation
> free time to walk outdoors in a lovely environment
> making or receiving a visible reminder of the experience

• *Days of prayer* • Before special events in the students' lives, celebrate a day of prayer. For instance, before First Holy Communion have a Jesus Day, before Confirmation have a Spirit Day, and before graduation have a Moving On Day. Prepare for these occasions by novenas of prayers and provide the families with suggested prayers to do so.

Sunday: the Holy Pause

Explain the meaning of the Sabbath or distribute a sheet about it. Include ideas from Illustration R, page 136, and the following notes.

The Sabbath

1. "Rest" in the Bible is *menuha*. This word is more active than our English word. It signifies purposeful contemplation, becoming quiet enough inside to see more deeply into life. It conveys the ideas of the good life, the absence of strife, inner tranquility, and the opportunity for reflection.
2. Sabbath rest allows us to see the big things in life that give everything else meaning. It helps us to realize who we are.
3. Jesus healed on the Sabbath. How do we use the Sabbath?
4. Sabbath is a day to worship; leisure alone becomes laziness.
5. Sabbath is a time to be open and vulnerable to the Spirit of God.
6. On the Sabbath we are to discover, appreciate, and enjoy life: our own life, the mystery of life, and the divine in life. We are to be with others and to be with Jesus.
7. Sabbath is not just the sixty minutes we spend at the Eucharist; it is the entire day, a little Easter on which we rest and celebrate resurrection.
8. Sabbath is a family day and a community day for the People of God.
9. Sabbath is a day to listen to God speak in creation and to seek creative ways to say to God, "I love you, too."
10. Sabbath is a day to re-create.
11. Sabbath is not a dumping day to do everything we didn't finish during the week; it is a day to wonder and to be, a day to float, to "kill time."
12. The great Sabbath is heaven: eternal rest.

Universe
as a Springboard for Prayer

LORD of heaven and earth, Creator of the waters, King of all you have created, hear my prayer!   Judith 9:12

When the astronauts of the Apollo 7 mission beheld our planet earth from space, they radioed back the words of Psalm 8:4-5:

> When I behold your heavens, the work of your fingers,
>   the moon and the stars which you set in place—
> What is man that you should be mindful of him,
>   or the son of man that you should care for him?

We don't have to be thousands of miles in space to be moved to prayer by creation. Standing on Earth looking into a star-spangled sky has the same effect. Through activities that use creation as a springboard to prayer, catechists can teach children to find God in creation. God is also present in every person and event in our lives. God is not aloof on some far planet in outer space. Rather, God is Emmanuel, God-with-us, now and forever. God is here on Earth watching, loving, and caring. Faith transforms occurrences in our daily lives as well as world events into opportunities to draw closer to God. The following activities awaken students to the reality of God in the world and show them how to find the supernatural through the natural.

Prayer from Nature
God is easily discovered in the marvelous works of creation that surround and awe us with their beauty, their intricacies, and their power.

• *A Nature walk* • Take your students on a nature walk. Lead them into prayer by having them join in a litany of praise as you go along:

> For jack-in-the-pulpits, we praise you, Lord.
> For fresh, cool breezes, we praise you, Lord.
> For sunlight and shadows, we praise you, Lord.
> For colorful butterflies, we praise you, Lord.

• *Prayer about an object* • Have the students bring one object from a nature walk like an acorn or a wildflower and write a prayer based on what they found.

• *"Canticle of Brother Sun"* • Pray with the students St. Francis of Assisi's "Canticle of Brother Sun." Accompany it with pictures or slides.

> Most high, all-powerful, all good, Lord!
>> All praise is yours, all glory, all honor
>> And all blessing.
> To you, alone, Most High, do they belong.
>> No mortal lips are worthy
>> To pronounce your name.
> All praise be yours, my Lord, through all that you have made,
>> And first my Lord Brother Sun,
>> Who brings the day; and light you give to us through him.
> How beautiful is he, how radiant in all his splendor!
>> Of you, Most High, he bears the likeness.
> All praise be yours, my Lord, through Sister Moon and Stars;
>> In the heavens you have made them, bright
>> And precious and fair.
> All praise be yours, my Lord, through Brothers Wind and Air,
>> And fair and stormy, all the weather's moods,
>> By which you cherish all that you have made.
> All praise be yours, my Lord, through Sister Water,
>> So useful, lowly, precious and pure.
> All praise be yours, my Lord, through Brother Fire,
>> Through whom you brighten up the night.
> How beautiful is he, how gay! Full of power and strength.
> All praise be yours, my Lord, through Sister Earth, our mother,
>> Who feeds us in her sovereignty and produces
>> Various fruits with colored flowers and herbs.
> All praise be yours, my Lord, through those who grant pardon
>> For love of you; through those who endure
>> Sickness and trial.
> Happy those who endure in peace,
>> By you, Most High, they will be crowned.
> All praise be yours, my Lord, through Sister Death,
>> From whose embrace no mortal can escape.
> Woe to those who die in mortal sin!
>> Happy those She finds doing your will!
>> The second death can do no harm to them.
> Praise and bless my Lord, and give him thanks,
>> And serve him with great humility.

• *Posters and slides* • Display beautiful nature posters or slides and invite the students to write a prayer about them.

• *Experiences* • Invite the students to tell of a place outside where they felt very close to God.

• *God's attributes* • Compile a list of God's attributes from analyzing creations that reflect their Maker, for instance, mountains: power, daisy: gentleness.

• *Prayers of created things* • Tell the students to suppose that all created things had the power to pray. Let them compose prayers that these inanimate objects and animals might pray. They might draw a picture to accompany the prayer. Use the book *Prayers from the Ark* by Carmen Gatsztold to introduce the activity.

• *Alphabetic psalms* • Some psalms are alphabetic: Each line begins with a letter of the Hebrew alphabet. Help students make their own psalm of praise for gifts in creation. Have them think of some created thing for each letter of the alphabet and compose a line or two praising God for it.

• *Sacred places* • Encourage students to find a quiet, secret spot outside where they can hear God speak to them. They might record in journals what they experienced while they spent time in this sacred place.

• *Murals or notecards* • Have the students design a mural on a bulletin board or make a set of notecards on the theme "All creation praise the Lord."

• *Objects in Jesus' life* • Assist the students in compiling a list of created things that played a role in the life of Jesus or that are used in the sacraments. Have them write meditations on these objects.

• *Music from nature* • Play music with a theme from nature as a background for prayer like "The Moldau" or "Appalachian Spring."

• *Images of God* • Present God to younger children using images from nature: a rainbow or their favorite blanket.

• *Seasonal prayers* • Invite the students to write a prayer for each season.

Prayer from Anything

Teach the students that anything can be a source of prayer. Give them an example. I like to use Berardo, a crocheted clown. An eighth-grade class discussed what clowns were and the purposes they served. They talked about their favorite clowns and this particular clown. Then they wrote prayers linked to these ideas. Here are some of them:

1. Stefanie writes a prayer of gratitude:
   Lord, thank you for all the clowns you give us, from the ones that talk to the ones that just act. From the clowns in school, to the clowns in a circus. They always make the day better and brighter no matter how bad of a day. I'd hate to see the world without smiles and laughter. Thanks for adding them to our world.

2. Andy ponders ways that God makes him happy:
    God you're always there to cheer me up when I feel down.
    When I'm tired and bored you're there to keep me going.
    When things become hard you're there to help me through.
    When I'm mad you're able to make me feel better.
    And when I'm sick you're there to help me get well again.

3. Nicole follows another track. She reflects on times when she is made fun of:
    God, thank you for giving me friends to help brighten my day when every-
    thing isn't going in the right direction. I feel comforted knowing that not
    everybody laughs at me when others joke about me. I'll always have my
    friends—and you there to help me through it all, to help me push on and
    not give up because of some person who thinks it's funny. Thank you.

4. Amy is led to reflect on God's attributes:
    I think this clown is like God because he makes people happy; so does God.
    The clown is jolly; so is God. The clown's jokes are also funny; so is God,
    sometimes. A clown is filled with laughter and joy and love toward others
    and that is what God does the best.

5. Anthony, too, thinks of God's attributes:
    You are always smiling, always joyful. I wonder how anyone would want to
    stray away from your beliefs. But if they do, you still smile at them and are
    always ready to take them back.

6. Luci writes a prayer of petition:
    Keep entertaining me. Let your pantomimes mold us into good. Let us make
    someone's day as cheerful as you make ours.

7. Chris writes an examination of conscience:
    When I look at that clown, I ask myself, "Am I really making others happy?"
    I ask myself over and over again. I'm really not sure. Sometimes I act on
    what other people tell me. I know it's what I shouldn't do. Tell me and help
    me know when I am not being the best person I can be. Let me know on the
    spot.

8. Becky, too, arrives at self-knowledge:
    Lord, I think that I should become more cheerful and help more people. I
    should try to stay in a good mood and make other people happy instead of
    somewhat miserable. I should set a better example to younger people also.

• *Objects from home* • Invite the students to bring an object to class and make it
the subject of a prayer.

• *Objects on cards* • Make a set of cards with the names of everyday objects written on them or pictures pasted on them. Have the students draw a card from a box

and write a prayer with the subject of the card suggesting the theme. Suggestions for cards: a tooth, a test, a field of wheat, a camel, a pencil, a book, a computer, a birthday cake, a clock.

Prayer from Experiences
God speaks and acts in our lives through everything that happens to us. The people we meet, ordinary daily routines, extraordinary crises—all have the potential to draw us closer to God.

• *Litany of thanksgiving* • Have students list their blessings and then use the list for a litany of thanksgiving.

• *Gratitude for four gifts* • Direct the students to divide a page into four sections, draw in each section a gift they have received from God, and then write a prayer of gratitude.

• *Prayer for concerns* • Ask the students to write their five greatest concerns or fears. Then have them check the ones they have actually prayed for by name. Invite them to reflect how often they have prayed about what really matters to them.

• *Personal experiences* • Share a story about a time you sensed God working in your life to bring about good. Encourage the students to share their personal experiences. Close with a prayer or song of praise and thanksgiving.

• *Bulletin board* • Create a bulletin board of world events that need prayer. Keep it up-to-date. Use it for class prayer.

• *A modern testament* • The Old Testament is a record of God's working in Hebrew history. The New Testament is the story of God's working in the first days of Christianity. Have the students write a third testament: a modern testament that is a record of God working in their parish, their neighborhood, or their country. Include events that are "good news" and accounts of people who are filled with the Holy Spirit.

• *Prayers from the news* • Distribute news sections of your daily newspaper. Have students compose prayers about certain news items. Pray them during a special prayer service for the world.

• *Journals* • Teach the students to keep a journal as an aid to interpreting their lives in the light of God's love and as a stepping-stone to prayer. (See "W: Writing and Journaling," page 97.)

• *Previews and reviews* • Instill in the students the habit of morning and evening prayer that focuses on their lives. In the morning they could preview the coming activities, offer them to God, and ask his blessing on them. In the evening they could review the day's happenings and express praise, thanks, or sorrow.

• *Commercials* • Challenge the students to collect slogans from commercials and ads that could be applied to God. Example: God cares enough to send the very best.

• *Daily events* • State things that could happen during the day and ask the students to suggest possible prayer responses. Sample events:
  You fail a test.
  A new friend comes to visit.
  A sibling wrecks a possession.
  You get sick.
  You lose your temper and talk back to your parent.
  You notice a lovely flower.
  You see someone cheating in school.

• *Healing of memories* • Lead students in exercises for the healing of memories. Have them recall times when they have been hurt or when they have hurt others. Help them to face these events in the presence of Jesus and ask him to heal them.

• *Collages of gifts* • Have the students make collages of the good things God has put in their lives. They might cover the inside of a gift box with pictures and words.

• *People who are blessings* • Tell the students to think of people they know and admire, living and dead. Have them list the Christ-like qualities of these people and then compose a prayer asking for these virtues for themselves.

• *Prayer for blessings* • Have the students write a prayer asking God's blessing on a person they like and a person they don't like or an enemy. Encourage them to pray their prayers.

• *School subjects* • Arrange the students in groups and have each group compose a prayer about one of their school subjects.

• *Prayer for the family* • Have the students compose a prayer for their family and pray it.

• *Prayer commitment* • Provide the students with a list of organizations or a list of missionaries. Let them choose one to support with prayer. They might wish to contact the people involved and inform them of their prayer commitment.

• *Prayer hands* • Have the students trace one of their hands and write in it needs for which they would like to pray.

Visuals
to Prompt and Aid Prayer

The fervent prayer of a righteous person is very powerful. James 5:16

A picture is worth a thousand words. Images and paintings have power to move our hearts. Visuals with religious themes and with secular themes can raise our thoughts to God and inspire prayer.

• *Poster or slide* • Show a poster or slide to the class. Discuss it and then invite the students to speak to God about it in their hearts. For instance, show a picture of a child resting on God's hand. Ask questions like:

> Whose hand is shown?
> Who does the child represent?
> What do you think the child feels like?
> What does the hand do for the child?
> Do you ever feel like the child in the picture?
> Would you like to feel like the child?

Then comment: Speak to God your Father about this picture...Recall signs of God's love in your life...Thank God for loving care...Ask God to help you remember that, no matter what, God loves you...Speak to God about any problem or concern you have right now....

• *Slides* • Use slides to accompany a prayer or meditation.

• *Doodles* • Have the students doodle on a sheet of paper, making curves and lines at random. Then tell them to look at the design and try to detect an object in it. Have them write prayers flowing from what they saw in their art.

• *A holy card* • Give the students a holy card with a picture on it. Have them hold it in their hands and reflect on it or use it to focus themselves on prayer.

• *Stained-glass windows* • Use stained-glass windows or slides of them to stimulate prayer. Invite the students to speak to God about the subject or event depicted in the window.

• *Icons* • Teach your students about icons, how they are made as an act of worship, and how they are used in prayer. Display an icon and lead the students to pray from it. Tell them to become aware of the presence the icon represents.

• *Pictures* • Have the students paste a postcard or a lovely picture from a magazine on a sheet of paper and then write a prayer to accompany it.

• *Psalm stations* • Have your students make psalm stations. Direct them to letter and decorate psalm verses on posters. Display the posters around the room and let the students pray them the way we pray the stations of the cross. You can do the same thing with proverbs, sayings of Jesus, and advice from the epistles.

• *Photos* • Ask your students to bring a favorite photo to school and compose a prayer to go with it.

• *Prayer cards* • Have the students make a prayer card for someone.

• *Object for focus* • Teach the students to use objects to focus their prayer: the tabernacle, a crucifix, or a statue.

• *A scene* • Have the students think of a scene that would put them in a prayerful frame of mind, a place where they would like to pray. Give them a large sheet of drawing paper and have them color or paint their scene. Before appropriate prayer experiences in class, have the students set this desk mat before them and imagine that they are there.

• *Pictures* • Give your students holy cards, pictures, and photos of art pieces to keep as launching pads for prayer.

• *Banners* • Use a banner displayed in church or put one up one in the classroom as a springboard for prayer. Have the students make their own banner or antependium (material that hangs in front of the altar). Let them design a banner on the computer.

• *Miscellaneous* • Have the students make buttons, badges, plaques, T-shirts, cups, bumper stickers, doorknob hangers, bookmarks, paperweights, or pennants that have messages about prayer or that inspire prayer.

Writing
and Journaling

*When you pray, go to your inner room, close the door, and pray to your Father in secret.
And your Father who sees in secret will repay you.*   Matthew 6:6

As an English teacher, I taught my students that you don't know what you think until you write it. As someone put it: "How can I know what I think until I see what I say?" Writing is a powerful way to stimulate thought and also to come to realizations about God, yourself, and life. It helps you find the door of your heart, and St. John Chrysostom said, "When you discover the door of your heart, you discover the gate of heaven."

Journaling

Begin to form the habit of journaling in the students by giving them class time to do it. There are different ways of handling journals in class. Some teachers check the activities and write comments to the students in their journals. Others regard the journals as strictly personal and never read them. Still others ask to read some parts and tell the students to paper clip the pages that are personal. Then they promise not to read these pages.

   If your budget allows, purchase books with blank pages, notebooks, or three-ring portfolios for each student. The students can decorate the covers.

• *An information sheet* • Give your students a sheet that describes the benefits and purposes of journaling. Include these ideas:

What is journaling?
The word *journal* comes from the French word for "day." A journal is a daily record. Journaling is a process by which we come to know ourselves, our deeper selves, the secret of who we are and what is possible for us.

A journal is
   a help to identify and communicate our needs and desires
   a place to go when things go wrong
   a record of the year, a life script
   a means to work through a confusing situation or bewildering feelings
   a place where you can be yourself
   a source of freedom, relaxation, and fun
   a step in resolving conflicts
   a gateway to growth

What can journaling do for you?

Lead you to realize and reflect on what you actually believe, think, fancy, and do

Challenge you to bring together religion and reality, personal values and life events

Help you to own your past and present more fully

Let you face life realistically

Nourish your personal growth

Heal wounds by letting you talk out hurtful situations

Change your self-concept

Inspire you to pray

How do you do journaling?

Set aside time for it. When you do not have time to make an entry, jot down key words on a special calendar.

Let it flow out of your mind and copy it down as it goes. Let it happen; don't force it, try to control it, or edit it.

Write about the day's experiences and your reactions.

Keep it private and be honest.

Reread your journal from time to time to see how God has spoken to you and how God has acted in your life. Thank God for love and guidance.

Topics for your journal: family, career goals, heroes, dreams, interests, death, Scripture events, news items, imaginary conversations.

• *Starters* • Provide starter questions and activities like the following to prime the pump for students' journaling.

Complete these sentences:

When I was little I believed...

I feel like a success/failure when...

I like/dislike...

I am proud/ashamed of...

I am happy/sad when...

It makes me angry when...

Sometimes I cry when...

I wish...

I don't care if...

The best thing about me is...

Nothing is as important to me as...

What kind of country are you: an island? a continent? landlocked? cold? rainy?

Recall a dream you had. What meaning does it have for you?

What do you usually daydream about?

Think of someone from your past and tell that person what he or she meant to you.
Who are your heroes?
What role does religion play in your life?
Draw a circle and inside it write or draw symbols for five things you value most.
Write the career you are thinking of going into and list your qualities and skills that
    would be helpful in it.
What is the happiest memory you have? the saddest?
What is your chief fault?
What do you get most excited about?
What is your least/most attractive physical feature?
Who would you most like to take a trip with?
What emotions are you feeling right now?
What are you most unwilling to write about right now?
What image of God do you like best?
What is the biggest challenge you face?
What do you and your parents argue about most?
What name would you choose for yourself?
What do you think God is saying to you now?

Other written prayers
• *A format* • Give students a prayer format to follow in writing original prayers.
They might follow the format of the opening prayers of Mass:

  1. Address God and say something to describe God or what God does.
  2. State a petition.
  3. Ask through the name of Jesus, who lives with the Father and the Holy Spirit.

• *A blank booklet* • Make blank prayer booklets for the students by folding and
stapling a few sheets of white paper together. Have them decorate the cover and fill
the booklet with prayers they find and like or original prayers.

• *Letter to God* • Have the students write a letter to God. Then have them write a
letter from God to them addressing them by name and signed "Love, God." They
might prefer to write to Jesus by name. The letter from God might be surprising
and revealing.

• *Conversation with God* • Tell the students to write a conversation with God.

• *Answering Jesus* • Direct the students to write their answer to a question that
Jesus poses in the Gospels:

    What are you looking for? (John 1:38)
    Do you want to be well? (John 5:6)
    Who do you say that I am? (Matthew 16:15)
    Why are you so terrified, O you of little faith? (Matthew 8:26)
    What do you want me to do for you? (Luke 18:41)
    Do you believe now? (John 16:31)

• *Written gospel meditations* • Here is a powerful and revealing prayer flowing from the gospel. Choose an event in which Jesus is present. Read the story and then write out a meditation following these steps:

1. Retell the story in your own words as if you were one of the people present during the incident described.
2. Conclude the story so that you and Jesus are alone together.
3. Write a conversation between you and Jesus about what occurred, leading into thoughts and feelings about yourself and what is happening in your life.

In Illustration S, page 138, is an example I wrote during a retreat. I used Luke 8:40-48, Jesus stopping to heal a woman on his way to Jairus's house. It will help you to know that I had just learned to drive and that in the retreat we had just finished a session on the capital sins.

Experience
of Prayer

Persevere in prayer, being watchful in it with thanksgiving. Colossians 4:2

Part of our task in teaching prayer is to convince the students that it is valuable—that it is necessary, and that it touches life. We lead them to realize that prayer, the interior life, is life's most intoxicating high, the peak experience. It can take them where drugs and alcohol cannot. In prayer they can find satisfaction, fulfillment, and peace. They will be dazzled by God.

• *Prayer packets* • Prepare, or have the students prepare for one another, a prayer experience using prayer packets. Assemble packets of materials on different themes containing prayers, pictures, cassette tapes, and anything else that could be used for at least three prayer activities. Include instructions. Have the students spend a class or part of a retreat choosing a packet and following the instructions.

Motivation
• *What prayer means to others* • Motivate your students to pray by having them hear what prayer means to other people. Invite witnesses to speak on prayer or have a panel of adults or older students talk about what prayer means to them. Give examples like the following:

Henri Nouwen describes vividly how necessary prayer is in his book *With Open Hands:* "The man who never prays...is like the child with asthma; because he is short of breath, the whole world shrivels up before him. He creeps in a corner gasping for air, and is virtually in agony. But the man who prays...is free to boldly stride through the world because he can move about without fear."

Abraham Lincoln said: "I have been driven many times to my knees by the overwhelming conviction that I had nowhere else to go. My wisdom, and that of all round me, seemed insufficient for the day."

George Washington Carver was a former slave who became a great scientist. He is famous for making 300 products from the peanut. When someone asked how he became so successful, he explained that he rose each morning at four o'clock and walked in the woods. He said, "In the woods, while most other persons are sleeping, I hear and understand God's plan for me."

• **What prayer meant to saints** • Teach how the saints always valued prayer, how the Indians called St. Rose Philippine Duchesne "the woman who always prays." You might relate the story of St. Thérèse's prayer. From her Carmelite cloister she prayed for the salvation of a hardened criminal. She was relieved to learn that as he approached his execution, he asked for the blessing of the priest.

• **Interviews** • Have the students interview their parents, their grandparents, their friends and neighbors, asking questions like, "How do you pray? When do you pray?" This assignment has the advantage of getting the students to talk to others on a deeper level.

• **Prayer stories** • Tell "prayer stories." Publications like *Catholic Digest, Guideposts,* and your own diocesan newspaper are good sources.

• **Personal experiences** • Share your own experiences with prayer—your successes and your difficulties. Even better, invite the students to share theirs. Once I asked the students in a ninth-grade CCD class to do this. One boy, Roger, told how he was alone by a pond one day, wondering if God was real. He prayed that God would give him a sign if he really existed. At that moment there was a splash in the pond. Roger believed that God had heard his prayer and had communicated with him. Now some might say, "That was a fish or a frog," but to Roger, that was God. I think Roger taught the class more that day than I did.

• **Breakdown of a lifetime** • Help the students put their life in perspective. Show them statistics like the following and have them figure out the amount of time they devote each day or week to other activities and to prayer.

> During 70 years of life we spend:
> 23 years sleeping
> 11 years working
> 8 years recreating
> 6 years eating
> 5 1/2 years grooming
> 3 years being educated
> 3 years reading
> 3 years talking
> 1/2 year worshiping God

• **Analysis of personal prayer** • Direct the students to write
   1. three of their greatest wishes,
   2. three things they are worried about right now,
   3. and then three wonderful things that happened to them lately.
Tell them to look at their lists and put a check next to those things that they have definitely prayed about. They will probably be surprised.

• **Prayer service** • Arrange a short prayer service to conclude and summarize each religion class. Invite the parents to it if they come to take your students home.

The Practice of Prayer

Throughout the centuries and across cultures, special postures accompany encounters with the Holy One. Moses removed his sandals before the burning bush, people fell to their knees before Jesus the Lord, Jews don their prayer shawls for prayer, and Muslims unroll their prayer mats and touch their foreheads to the floor. Practices like these signal a change of focus from this world to the spiritual realm and prepare us psychologically for prayer.

• *Posture* • Teach the different postures for prayer listed here and suggest that the students experiment with them. Encourage the students to be comfortable enough so that the body doesn't interfere with praying. Point out that having a straight back facilitates prayer. Explain to children that their backbone is made of a lot of little bones. They should sit so that the bones are stacked on top of one another.

Postures for Prayer

Standing—a sign of dignity, respect, and readiness

Sitting—allows you to relax and enjoy the presence of God

Kneeling—expresses adoration and penance

Bowing—shows humble submission and adoration

Lying flat on your back—a comfortable way St. Ignatius liked to pray

Prostrating—expresses total adoration; the prone position deacons assume
during the sacrament of holy orders

Sitting in a lotus pose—practiced by Orientals for meditation: sit on the floor
or a cushion; cross legs at the calves so that feet rest at the bend of
the knees; rest hands on heels with forefingers and thumbs touching to
form a circle

Sitting crosslegged—simpler than a lotus pose

Walking—a slow, thoughtful walk

Holding arms outstretched

Resting hands opened on lap, palms up

Holding hands with others

• *Preventing distractions* • In class tell the students to close their eyes and put their heads down if they wish, to eliminate distractions and better use their imaginations. Stand in the back of the room so that the students feel more comfortable.

• *Genuflecting* • A little boy went to church with his aunt. As they walked down the aisle, the aunt leaned down and whispered, "Can you genuflect?" "No," the boy replied, "but I can somersault." Teach little children to show reverence for the Blessed Sacrament by genuflecting on the right knee and without holding onto the pew.

Relaxing Exercises to Prepare for Prayer

• *Breathing* • Teach the students to do breathing exercises to relax before praying. Tell them to inhale slowly, count to five, and then exhale slowly, concentrating on their breathing. Have them repeat this three times.

• *Awareness* • Simply have the students listen to their breathing or be conscious of their heartbeat.

• *Muscles* • Teach the students to relax their muscles before prayer. Have them begin with the top of their head, tightening the muscles there for a few seconds and then loosening them. Then have them focus in turn on their forehead, their eyes, their mouth, their cheeks, neck, shoulders, arms, hands, chest, thighs, lower legs, and feet, each time tightening and then loosening the muscles.

• *Sensations* • Tell the students to be aware of the sensations different parts of their bodies are feeling. For instance, have them sense the temperature of the air in the room on their arms, the feeling of the chair beneath them, the touch of their shoes on their feet.

• *Floating* • Have the students imagine they are floating on a cloud or on a river.

• *Mantras* • Give the students a word or phrase to use as a mantra. Have them repeat it for a while before entering into a prayer activity. They might use their own name and imagine that God is calling them. Other suggestions:

    God.   My God and my All.
    Jesus. My Jesus, mercy.
    Abba.   My God, I love you.
            Maranatha ("Come, Lord Jesus.")

• *Soothing recordings* • Use audiotapes of soothing or uplifting music like "Chariots of Fire" or "Rachel's Song" for an introduction to prayer or as background. Purchase or make tapes of sounds from nature: waves, birdsong, or a running stream.

The Habit of Prayer
• *Prayer throughout the day* • Discuss ways people have of remembering to pray throughout the day: holy pictures displayed in their homes, church bells, praying at the sound of sirens, saying "God bless you."

• *Survey of habits* • Conduct a personal survey of prayer habits in which the students write the answers to questions like the following and then share them with another person or a small group:

    When do you pray? Where? How often?
    What prayers have you memorized?
    What was the first prayer you learned?
    When was the last time you prayed?
    Why did you pray?
    What is your favorite place for prayer?
    What is your favorite time for prayer?

What prayers do you like to pray?
What are concerns or fears in your life right now?
Have you prayed about them?
How do you usually pray?

• *Set times* • Encourage the students to have a set time for prayer instead of praying only when they feel like it. Explain two of the best times: early in the morning before the world comes alive and their minds are uncluttered by the concerns of the day, and in the evening when the day's activities are ended and they are preparing to sleep.

• *A log* • Suggest to the students that in forming the habit of daily prayer, they might record the times they remember to pray. Give them a sheet which they can use as a log to keep track of the times they prayed.

• *A checklist* • Give the students a leaflet of questions to use as a check-up of their prayer life. See Illustration T, page 139.

• *Meditation kit* • Use a meditation kit to develop the habit of prayer as Patricia Brisson describes in an issue of *Religion Teacher's Journal*. Each week a different student takes the kit home. The kit is a large pencil case that contains a crucifix, a notebook, and a three-minute egg timer. In the front of the notebook are these directions:

1. Find a quiet spot where you can be alone and not be disturbed. Sit in a comfortable position.
2. Choose a phrase on which to meditate. See suggestions below.
3. Write today's date and your meditation choice in the notebook.
4. Hold the crucifix in your hand or place it where you can see it.
5. Recall that you are in God's presence.
6. Turn over the timer and begin.
7. At the end of the week write one or two sentences telling what you thought or felt about the meditations. Was three minutes long enough? Did you feel as though you were really praying? Do you think it helped you? Would you like to do it again? Was it boring or too long? Please be honest.

Suggested prayer phrases:
>Thank you, Lord.
>Forgive me, Lord.
>I praise you, Jesus.
>I love you, Jesus.
>What should I do, Lord?

Yes

the Primary Attitude

Father...not my will but yours be done. Luke 22:42

The only prayer in the gospels that wasn't answered was Jesus' prayer in the Garden of Olives. But in the course of his praying, through blood, sweat, and tears, Jesus came to accept his Father's plan. Jesus is the model for our prayer. He prayed for something but then left the situation in the hands of his all-knowing and all-loving Father. Mary, too, assumed the stance of a handmaid before God. She was ready to cooperate in seeing that God's will be done whatever it exacted of her personally. In the Our Father, we pray "Thy will be done." If we are truly in love with God, in all of our prayer our mental frame will always be "Yes." We will not only accept God's will, but embrace it. In faith we pray with Dag Hammarskjold:

For all that has been—Thanks!
For all that shall be—Yes!

• *Three types of prayer* • Share with the students three types of prayers:

I am a bow in your hands, Lord.
Draw me, lest I rot.

Do not overdraw me, Lord.
I shall break.

Overdraw me,
and who cares if I break!

• *God's answer* • Discuss how God answers. Warn the students that sometimes God says No. Let them discuss why. Give the following examples:

From Archbishop Anthony Bloom: A child once prayed that he would be given the amazing gift his uncle had—every evening he took his teeth out of his mouth and put them in a glass of water. When the child grew up he was terribly happy that God hadn't granted his wish.

I asked for health, that I might do greater things;
   I was given infirmity, that I might do better things.
I asked for riches, that I might be happy;
   I was given poverty, that I might be wise.
I asked for power, that I might have the praise of men;
   I was given weakness, that I might feel the need of God.
I asked for all things, that I might enjoy life;
   I was given life, that I might enjoy all things.
I got nothing I asked for, but everything I hoped for.
Almost despite myself, my unspoken prayers were answered.
I am among all men, most richly blessed.

Explain that God sometimes answers in ways we don't expect. Tell the story of the man during a flood. He had climbed onto the roof of his house, but the waters were rising. He prayed to the Lord to deliver him from the flood. A rowboat went by and his neighbors called and invited him in. He waved them on saying, "No, I'm trusting in the Lord." A while later a motorboat stopped. Again the man said, "No thanks. I'm trusting in the Lord." Finally, the waters were still rising, and a helicopter flew over. The man waved them on too, saying, "I'm trusting in the Lord." The man drowned and went to heaven. When he met the Lord, he asked, "I prayed to you. Why didn't you answer me?" The Lord replied, "I sent you a rowboat, a motorboat, and a helicopter. What more did you want?"

• *Mary as model of prayer* • Present Mary's "Fiat" as a model. Discuss what her commitment to God's will demanded of her.

• *God's will* • Tell the students that in prayer we do not try to change God's will but to understand God's will. Prayer is not a way to make our will be done.

• *Prayer of Abandonment* • Teach Charles de Foucauld's Prayer of Abandonment that clearly expresses the attitude of surrender to God's will:

Father, I abandon myself into your hands; do with me what you will. Whatever you may do, I thank you: I am ready for all, I accept all. Let only your will be done in me, and in all your creatures—I wish no more than this, O Lord. Into your hands I commend my soul; I offer it to you with all the love of my heart, for I love you, Lord, and so need to give myself, to surrender myself into your hands, without reserve, and with boundless confidence, for you are my Father.

Z

Z-Z-Z
Sleep and Other Obstacles to Prayer

Could you not keep watch for one hour? Mark 14:37

Many people long to pray, but their wishes are never realized. They are defeated by obstacles to prayer: misconceptions about what prayer is, seeming lack of time, distractions, discouragement, and sleepiness. Hubert van Zeller wrote, "A lot of the trouble about prayer would disappear if we only realized—really realized, and not just supposed that it was so—that we go to pray not because we love prayer but because we love God."

• *Letters for advice* • Have the students write letters about problems in prayer as if to Ann Landers. Collect the letters and distribute them randomly to the students. Let each student answer the letter, giving advice to the classmate. Have the letters and their answers read aloud.

Misconceptions about Prayer
Dispel for your students three misconceptions about prayer: that it's long, that to be good it must give us many good thoughts, and that it should be formal.

• *Prayer needn't be long.* • A classic book on prayer, *The Cloud of Unknowing*, says that short prayer pierces the heavens. The book gives the example of a man whose house is on fire. When he realized it, he doesn't compose a lengthy sentence. (A conflagration is devastating my house, so would someone please come to my assistance?) He just yells, "Fire!" St. Augustine said, "A long speech is one thing, a long love another."

• *We don't have to get many good ideas from prayer.* • What teenager after a date says, "I had a really good time. Look at all the notes I took on what my date said." Perhaps the grace that comes from prayer is not an idea at all, but a moment of joy, a tear in the eye, a desire, or a resolution.

• *Prayer doesn't have to be stilted or solemn.* • St. Teresa advised, "Try not to let the prayer you make to such a Lord be mere politeness...avoid being bashful with God." Recall how Tevye talks with God in *Fiddler on the Roof*. Plain, sincere, loving words mean more than multisyllabic words said merely out of a sense duty. We should be as comfortable with God as the little girl who was learning to ride the bicycle and prayed, "Lord, if you'll give me a push, I'll do all the pedaling."

Seeming Lack of Time

Someone once said, "If you are too busy for prayer, you are too busy."

• *Discussion* • Discuss the statement, "We can always find time to do the things we want." Conclude that if we value prayer, we will plan for it. We will allow prayer to happen in us. Tell the students that someone once said, "The easiest way to find time to do all the things you want is to turn off the TV."

• *Short prayers* • Suggest ways to pray that take little or no time: a thought or short prayer to God during the day.

• *Odd moments* • Propose ways to pray that use odd moments in the day and ask the students for other examples:

1. Pray while you are on hold on the phone and listening to the music.
2. When tempted to charge through a yellow caution light, stop instead and pray while waiting for the red light to change.
3. Pray while standing in a checkout line.
4. Pray while waiting for a bus.

There are times when we really don't have time to pray. Tell the students this story: A cobbler asked his rabbi, "What can I do about my morning prayer? My customers are poor people who have only one pair of shoes. I pick up their shoes late in the evening and work on them most of the night so the people have them before they go to work. Sometimes I rush through prayer and get back to work. Other times I skip my hour of prayer. Then I feel bad, and every now and then as I work I can almost hear my heart sigh, 'What an unlucky man I am that I am not able to make my morning prayer.'" The rabbi answered, "If I were God, I would value that sigh more than the prayer."

Distractions

• *Explanation* • Explain to the students that it's natural, though frustrating, to have distractions flying around in our brain like gnats while we're trying to pray. Tell them the story of the man who promised a friend that he would give him his horse if the friend could get through saying the Our Father without a distraction. The friend, thinking this was an easy way to win a horse, began to pray, "Our Father, who art in heaven." Suddenly he stopped and asked, "Do I get the saddle too?"

• *Tips* • Share with the students some tips for combating distractions:

1. Sit on the edge of a chair with your spine straight.
2. Focus on an object near you.
3. Use a mantra, a word or phrase, to call you back to prayer.
4. Transform your distraction into a prayer: incorporate it in your prayer by expressing gratitude or a plea for help.

• *Possible meaning* • Explain to the students that sometimes a distraction may be a problem we need to deal with in our life. God calls our attention to it in prayer as a means to prod us into action.

Discouragement

• *Explanation* • Tell your students that the test of true prayer is not how good it makes us feel—but if we're doing God's will better. Point out that God's presence and love do not depend on our moods. God is with us whether we sense it or not.

• *Prayer for prayer* • Let your students know that one of the things they can pray for is the gift of prayer.

• *The Holy Spirit* • Remind the students that the Holy Spirit present within them prays in them. Read aloud Romans 8:26-27.

• *Tip* • Suggest that when the students don't feel like praying, during "periods of dryness," it might help to pray ready-made prayers.

• *An encouraging quotation* • Read to the students Julian of Norwich's words on prayer from her writings called *Revelation*:

> Our Lord is greatly cheered by our prayer. He looks for it, and he wants it...So he says, "Pray inwardly, even if you do not enjoy it. It does you good, though you feel nothing, see nothing, yes even though you think you are dry, empty, sick or weak. At such a time your prayer is most pleasing to me."

• *God's desire* • Tell the students that there is something far greater than our desire to pray: God's desire that we pray. Read the poem "The Hound of Heaven" by Francis Thompson.

Sleepiness

• *St. Thérèse's explanation* • Tell the students that St. Thérèse of Lisieux explained that she did not regret sleeping during prayer. She recalled that little children please their parents as much when they sleep as when they are awake. She also pointed out that when doctors operate they put patients to sleep. The heavenly Father loves us as we sleep.

• *The right time* • Recommend to the students that they find a prayer time when they are wide awake.

• *Prevention* • Suggest eating a candy bar or drinking coffee before praying.

Illustration A (for page 13)

Blessed are you when they insult you and persecute you and utter every kind of evil against you [falsely] because of me.
Matthew 5:11

I say to you, love your enemies, and pray for those who persecute you.
Matthew 5:44

Your light must shine before others, that they may see your good deeds and glorify your heavenly Father.
Matthew 5:16

If you bring your gift to the altar, and there recall that your brother has anything against you, leave your gift there at the altar, go first and be reconciled with your brother, and then come and offer your gift.
Matthew 5:23-24

Be perfect, just as your heavenly Father is perfect.
Matthew 5:48

When you pray, go to your inner room, close the door, and pray to your Father in secret.
Matthew 6:6

Do not store up for yourselves treasures on earth, where moth and decay destroy, and thieves break in and steal. But store up treasures in heaven.
Matthew 6:19-20

Look at the birds in the sky; they do not sow or reap, they gather nothing into barns, yet your heavenly Father feeds them. Are not you more important than they?
Matthew 6:26

Ask and it will be given to you; seek and you will find; knock and the door will be opened to you.
Matthew 7:7

Do to others whatever you would have them do to you.
Matthew 7:12

Stop judging, that you may not be judged.
Matthew 7:1

Do not be afraid of those who kill the body but cannot kill the soul; rather, be afraid of the one who can destroy both soul and body.
Matthew 10:28

Come to me, all you who labor and are burdened, and I will give you rest.
Matthew 11:28

If you have faith the size of a mustard seed, you will say to this mountain, "Move from here to there," and it will move. Nothing will be impossible for you.
Matthew 17:20

"Lord, if my brother sins against me, how often must I forgive him? As many as seven times?" Jesus answered, "I say to you, not seven times but seventy times seven."
Matthew 18:21-22

Whoever wishes to be great among you shall be your servant.
Matthew 20:26

Do not be afraid; just have faith.
Mark 5:36

I am the resurrection and the life; whoever believes in me, even if he dies, will live.
John 11:25-26

In the world you will have trouble, but take courage, I have conquered the world.
John 16:33

Blessed are those who have not seen and have believed.
John 20:29

Love your enemies; do good to those who hate you.
Luke 6:27

Be merciful, just as [also] your Father is merciful.
Luke 6:36

Whoever wishes to come after me must deny himself, take up his cross, and follow me.
Mark 8:34

The LORD is my shepherd; I shall not want. Psalm 23:1

Relieve the troubles of my heart, and bring me out of my distress. Psalm 25:17

The Lord is my light and my salvation; whom should I fear? Psalm 27:1

Those who seek the LORD want for no good thing. Psalm 34:11

O LORD, your kindness reaches to heaven. Psalm 36:6

Cast your care upon the LORD, and he will support you. Psalm 55:23

You have done great things; O God, who is like you? Psalm 71:19

Better a poor man who walks in his integrity than he who is crooked in his ways and rich. Proverbs 28:6

A faithful friend is a sturdy shelter; he who finds one finds a treasure. Sirach 6:14

We are the clay and you the potter: we are all the work of your hands. Isaiah 64:7

Fear not, for I have redeemed you; I have called you by name: you are mine. Isaiah 43:1

When you pass through the water, I will be with you; in the rivers you shall not drown. When you walk through fire, you shall not be burned; the flames shall not consume you. Isaiah 43:2

See, I place my words in your mouth! Jeremiah 1:9

Blessed is the man who trust in the LORD, whose hope is the LORD. He is like a tree planted beside the waters that stretches out its root to the stream. Jeremiah 17:7-8

God, my Lord, is my strength; he makes my feet swift as those of hinds and enables me to go upon the heights. Habakkuk 3:19

All things work for good for those who love God. Romans 8:28

Do not repay anyone evil for evil; be concerned for what is noble in the sight of all. Romans 12:17

Do nothing out of selfishness or out of vain glory; rather, humbly regard others as more important than yourselves. Philippians 2:3

Let anyone who thirsts come to me and drink. John 7:37

This is my commandment: love one another even as I love you. John 15:12

Blessed are those who have not seen and have believed. John 20:29

...affliction produces endurance, and endurance, proven character, and proven character, hope, and hope does not disappoint, because the love of God has been poured out into our hearts through the holy Spirit. Romans 5:3-5

If the Spirit of the one who raised Jesus from the dead dwells in you, the one who raised Christ from the dead will give life to your mortal bodies also. Romans 8:11

Be firm, steadfast, always fully devoted to the work of the Lord, knowing that in the Lord your labor is not in vain. 1 Corinthians 15:58

God loves a cheerful giver. 2 Corinthians 9:7

Be kind to one another, compassionate, forgiving one another as God has forgiven you in Christ. Ephesians 4:32

Illustration B (for page 16)

Meditation on Blind Bartimaeus
Mark 10:46-52

Still the body: Quiet yourself. Relax. Listen to your breathing.

Quiet the mind: Put everything out of your mind—what you're going to eat at your next meal, what you will do when you get home. Think only of Jesus, present here, loving you, waiting to speak to you.

Read the scriptural passage: Read Mark 10:46-52 slowly.

Recreate the story: See Bartimaeus sitting at the side of the road. He has a cup for money and a crude staff. His eyes are milky and unseeing, and his beard is scraggly. He is wearing sandals and ragged clothes. Whenever he hears people coming, Bartimaeus raises his cup and begs for alms. Suddenly, people surround him, talking excitedly, waiting for someone. "What's going on?" Bartimaeus asks. "Jesus of Nazareth is coming this way," someone replies. Bartimaeus says, "Jesus!" He cries out, "Jesus, son of David, have pity on me!" Again and again he calls. People at his side say, "Be quiet. Stop your noise." But Bartimaeus cries even louder, "Jesus, son of David, have pity on me."

Jesus is coming down the road with his disciples and a crowd of men, women, and children. He hears his name and stops. He says to the crowd, "Tell him to come here." People say to blind Bartimaeus, "Get up. He's calling you." Bartimaeus throws off his ragged cloak and jumps up. He staggers in the direction of Jesus' voice. Jesus asks, "What do you want me to do for you?" Bartimaeus answers, "Master, I want to see." Jesus replies, "Go your way; your faith has saved you." All of a sudden Bartimaeus can see the face of Jesus looking at him. He can see the astonished people around him. He can see the the sky, the grass, the dusty road. He is thrilled. He joins the crowd following Jesus. People keep coming up to Bartimaeus and asking, "How did he do it?"

Reflect on the story: Bartimaeus was blind. We, too, are blind in certain ways. We don't understand the mysteries of life. Maybe we don't see the marvelous things God is doing in our life . . . the love God has for us . . . and the love of others for us. We may be blind to our own faults . . . to dangers that we allow in our lives . . . to ways that we are hurting others. What might you be blind to in your life? [*Pause.*]

The secret to having sight is to call on God. Prayer helps us to see things as they really are, to see ourselves and others as God sees us. Like Bartimaeus we recognize Jesus, the Son of God, and cry out to him in our blindness and poverty. When voices, inside and out, tell us not to pray, not to turn to God for help, we ignore them and double our efforts to reach him. And Jesus will hear us and invite us to come to him. Eagerly we throw off our cloak, anything that might slow us down, and run to Jesus. Then we will begin to see. Who or what keeps you from praying? [*Pause.*]

Once we meet God and experience his healing love, we will never want to leave him. Dazzled by the light of his love, we will follow him to the ends of the earth and do whatever he wishes. How can you spend more time with Jesus? [*Pause.*]

Respond to Scripture: Talk to Jesus about a blind spot in your life. Is there anything you can do about it with his help? You might talk to Jesus about your prayer habits. How can you improve the time you spend knowing and loving God? How can you follow Jesus down the road more closely?

Illustration C (for page 20)

Prayer of the Heart: A Short Play

Background: Father Jim took the officers of St. Mary's youth club to a cottage for the weekend to plan the year's activities. After a day of brainstorming and swimming in the lake, the group sat on the beach and began to talk about prayer.

Characters: Father Jim, Amy, Gina, Tim, Paul

Tim: This has been a great day! I feel really close to God here.

Amy: Me, too. Closer than when I pray my night prayers or the rosary.

Gina: Father Jim, what's your favorite kind of prayer?

Father: Well, Gina, I'd have to say centering prayer.

Paul: Centering prayer—what's that? Is there a St. Centering I don't know about?

Father: No, Paul. Centering prayer is an ancient form of prayer that is popular again. It takes its name from the fact that in doing it, you center all your thoughts and feelings on God, who lives in the center of your being.

Tom: How do you do that?

Father: Do you really want to know?

All: Sure. Yes.

Father: OK. The first step is to quiet down, close your eyes, and think of God within you. You empty your mind of all other thoughts and pictures.

Tim: That ought to be easy for Gina. Her mind's pretty empty already.

Gina: Quiet, Tim. I want to hear this.

Father: As I was saying, you think of God, believe in him, and love him. You ask God to let you experience his presence, love, and care.

Paul: How long does this take?

Father: Just about a minute. Once you're in God's presence, you just rest there, responding to his love with love. You use a prayer word or phrase to keep your mind on Jesus.

Amy: What's a prayer word?

Father: A prayer word is a word or phrase that expresses your feelings for God. You can probably think of one yourself.

Gina: Well, when my sister talks in her sleep, she just says her boyfriend's name over and over. But I think I'll say "Jesus" as my prayer word.

Father: Wonderful. You repeat this word in your mind while you enjoy God's presence. You say it whenever other things come into your mind. It will bring your thoughts back to Jesus.

Gina: Don't you think about anything else during this prayer—like a gospel story or a problem you have?

Father: No, you just give God loving attention and let God surround you with the ocean of love. It's something like the swimming you did today.

Gina: That sounds beautiful.

Father: It is. It is so beautiful that you should end this prayer gradually, perhaps by praying a prayer like the Our Father slowly.

Paul: Otherwise it's like suddenly having the lights turned on when you've been in the dark.

Father: You've got it.

Amy: I don't think this prayer's for me. Sounds like the deep stuff the gurus do.

Father: It's really simple, Amy. Just give yourself to God and rest in God. It's like a child on a parent's lap. The parent is so happy the child is showing love that it doesn't matter if the child says nothing or even falls asleep.

Amy: I see. The important thing is that you're spending time with your friend, giving yourself to God.

Father: Exactly.

Tim: Why don't we plan a day of recollection for the club and teach everyone centering prayer?

Father: Good idea, Tim. But don't you think you'd better try it yourself first?

Gina: What's stopping us from doing it now?

Father: Nothing. Let's pray.

Illustration D (for page 27)

Outline of the Mass

Introductory Rites
    Entrance Procession and Song
    S _____ and Greeting
    Penitential Rite
    G _____ to _____
    Opening Prayer

Liturgy of the Word
    First Reading
        Responsorial P_____
    Second Reading
        Gospel Acclamation
    G _____
    H _____
    Profession of F _____
    General Intercessions

Liturgy of the Eucharist
    Preparation of the Altar and Gifts
        Prayer over the Gifts
    Eucharistic Prayer
        P _____
        Holy, Holy, Holy Lord
        Institution Narrative and Consecration
        Offering
        Great A _____
    Communion Rite
        Lord's Prayer
        Sign of _____
        Breaking of the Bread: Lamb of God
        C _____
        Prayer after Communion

Concluding Rite
    B _____
    Dismissal

Answers: Sign of the Cross, Glory to God, Psalm, Gospel, Homily, Faith, Preface, Amen, Peace, Communion, Blessing

Illustration E (for page 28)

Plans for the Celebration of the Eucharist

Theme: _____ Date: _____
Celebrant:_____ Coordinator: _____

Opening hymn: _____

Glory to God: recited _____ sung ____ : _____

First reading: _____ read by _____

Responsorial psalm: recited_____ sung ____ : _____
        antiphon recited: _____ sung ____: _____

Second reading: _____ read by _____

Gospel acclamation: recited _____ sung ____ : _____

Gospel reading: _____

Prayer of the faithful: read by_____
        response:_____

Procession with gifts: wine: _____ hosts: _____
        other:_____

Hymn: _____

Holy, Holy, Holy: recited_____ sung _____ : _____

Memorial acclamation:_____ recited ____ sung _____

Great Amen: recited ____ sung ____

Our Father: recited ____ sung ____ : _____

Sign of peace: _____

Communion hymn: _____

Thanksgiving: recited ____ sung ____ : _____
        silence ____ other:_____

Closing hymn: _____

Illustration F (for page 29)

Eucharistic Word Search

Name:_____

Find and circle the 38 words listed below. They are hidden vertically, horizontally, and diagonally. Put a check before each word as you find it.

```
P I N T E R C E S S I O N S G S H C U P
C E L E B R A T I O N W A X C O O U L W
H O T I M N S C W B L I N W O R S H I P
U C H O T V A A I R R N O S M N T P R A
R Y A S T U C O C O L E T I M U P R E L
C C N N S I R U L R I F A Y U P R E L L
H R K D D T A G L A I A H D N O O F P E
J E S U S L M O Y G I F M O I D C A A L
O M G E L I E L P O M S I E O T E C S U
Q U I N C E N S E E E M L C N O S E S I
T R V L E C T I O N A R Y S E T S O O A
P B I X U V A X T R L C R E E D I C V L
C O N S E C R A T I O N E B L O O D E T
N D G E T A Y C H A S U B L E I N O R A
M Y S T E R Y I E N B L E S S I N G O R
```

alleluia
altar
amen
blessing
blood
body
bread
candles
celebration
chasuble
Church
communion
consecration

creed
cup
gifts
Gloria
Gospel
host
hymns
incense
intercessions
Jesus
Lectionary
liturgy
meal

mercy
mystery
Passover
peace
preface
priest
procession
Sacramentary
sacrifice
thanksgiving
wine
worship

Answers to Eucharistic Word Search

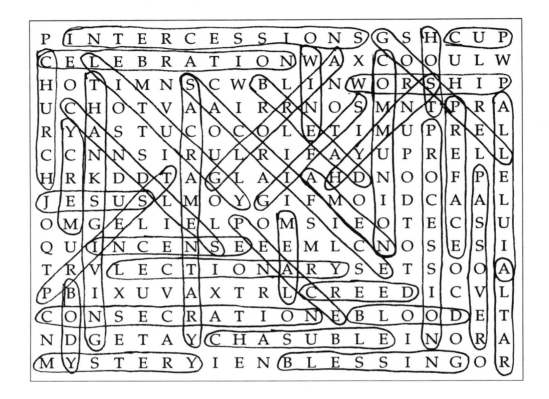

```
P I N T E R C E S S I O N S G S H C U P
C E L E B R A T I O N W A X C O O U L W
H O T I M N S C W B L I N W O R S H I P
U C H O T V A A I R R N O S M N T P R A
R Y A S T U C O L E T I M U P R E L L
C C N N S I R U L R I F A Y U P R E L L
H R K D D T A G L A I A H D N O O F P E
J E S U S L M O Y G I F M O I D C A S L
O M G E L I E L P O M S I E O T E C S U
Q U I N C E N S E E M L C N O S E O I A
T R V L E C T I O N A R Y S E T S O A
P B I X U V A X T R L C R E E D I C V L
C O N S E C R A T I O N E B L O O D E T
N D G E T A Y C H A S U B L E I N O R A
M Y S T E R Y I E N B L E S S I N G O R
```

120

Illustration G (for page 41)

One Solitary Life

He was born in an obscure village.
He worked in a carpenter shop until he was thirty.
He then became an itinerant preacher.
He never held an office.
He never had a family or owned a house.
He didn't go to college.
He had no credentials but himself.

He was only thirty-three when the public turned against him.
His friends ran away.
He was turned over to his enemies
and went through the mockery of a trial.
He was nailed to a cross between two thieves.
While he was dying, his executioners gambled for his clothing,
the only property he had on earth.
He was laid in a borrowed grave.
Nineteen centuries have come and gone,
and today he is the central figure of the human race.

All the armies that ever marched,
all the navies that ever sailed,
all the parliaments that ever sat,
and all the kings that ever reigned,
have not affected life on earth as much as that
one solitary life.

Illustration H (for page 41)

Desiderata
Found in Old St. Paul's Church, Baltimore, Maryland, 1692

Go placidly amid the noise and haste, and remember what peace there may be in silence. As far as possible without surrender, be on good terms with all persons. Speak your truth quietly and clearly; and listen to others, even the dull and ignorant; they too have their story. Avoid loud and aggressive persons; they are vexations to the spirit. If you compare yourself with others, you may become vain and bitter; for always there will be greater and lesser persons than yourself. Enjoy your achievements as well as your plans. Keep interested in your own career, however humble; it is a real possession in the changing fortunes of time. Exercise caution in your business affairs, for the world is full of trickery. But let this not blind you to what virtue there is; many persons strive for high ideals, and everywhere life is full of heroism.

Be yourself. Especially, do not feign affection. Neither be cynical about love, for in the face of all aridity and disenchantment it is perennial as the grass. Take kindly the counsel of the years, gracefully surrendering the things of youth. Nurture strength of spirit to shield you in sudden misfortune, but do not distress yourself with imaginings. Many fears are born of fatigue and loneliness.

Beyond a wholesome discipline, be gentle with yourself. You are a child of the universe, no less than the trees and the stars; you have a right to be here. And whether or not it is clear to you, no doubt the universe is unfolding as it should. Therefore, be at peace with God, whatever you conceive him to be, and whatever your labors and aspirations, in the noisy confusion of life keep peace with your soul. With all its sham, drudgery, and broken dreams, it is still a beautiful world.

Illustration I (for page 41)

Footprints

One night a man had a dream. He was walking along the beach with the Lord. Across the sky flashed scenes from his life. In each scene he noticed two sets of footprints in the sand: one belonging to him, and the other to the Lord.

When the last scene of his life flashed before him, he looked back at the footprints in the sand. He noticed that many times along the path of his life there was only one set of footprints. He also noticed that it happened at the very lowest and saddest times in his life.

This really bothered him, and he questioned the Lord about it. "Lord, you said that once I decided to follow you, you'd walk with me all the way. But I have noticed that during the most troublesome times in my life, there was only one set of footprints. I don't understand why, when I needed you most, you would leave me."

The Lord replied, "My precious, precious child, I love you and I would never leave you. During your times of trial and suffering, when you saw only one set of footprints, it was then that I carried you."

Letter from a Friend

Dear Friend,

I just had to send a note to tell you how much I love you and care about you. I saw you yesterday as you were walking with your friends. I waited all day, hoping you would want to talk with me also. As evening drew near, I gave you a sunset to close your day and a cool breeze to rest you. And I waited. But you never came. It hurt me, but I still love you because I am your friend.

I saw you fall asleep last night and I longed to touch your brow. So, I spilled moonlight on your pillow and your face. Again, I waited, wanting to rush down so that we could talk. I have so many gifts for you. But you awakened late the next day and rushed off to school. My tears were in the rain.

Today you looked so sad, so all alone. It makes my heart ache because I understand. My friends let me down and hurt me so many times, too. But I love you. Oh, if you would only listen to me. I really love you. I try to tell you in the blue sky and in the quiet green grass. I whisper it in the leaves on the trees and breathe it in the colors of the flowers. I shout it to you in the mountain streams and give the birds love songs to sing. I clothe you with warm sunshine and perfume the air with nature's scents. My love for you is deeper than the oceans and bigger than the biggest want or need in your heart.

If only you knew how much I want to help you. I want you to meet my Father. He wants to help you, too. My Father is that way, you know. Just call me, ask me, talk with me. I have so much to share with you. But, I won't hassle you. I'll wait because I love you.

Your friend,
Jesus

Illustration K (for page 41)

Persons Are Gifts

Persons are gifts!
Persons are gifts which the Father sends me wrapped!
Some are wrapped very beautifully;
they are very attractive when I first see them.
Some come in very ordinary wrapping paper.
Others have been mishandled in the mail.
Once in a while there is a "Special Delivery!"
Some persons are gifts which come very loosely wrapped;
others are wrapped very tightly.

But the wrapping is not the gift!
It is so easy to make this mistake.
Sometimes the gift is very easy to open up.
Sometimes I need others to help.
Is it because they are afraid?
Is it because we are afraid?
Does it hurt?
Maybe they have been opened up before and thrown away!
Could it be that the gift is not for me?

I am a person. Therefore I am a gift, too!
A gift to myself first of all.
The Father gave myself to me.
Have I ever really looked inside the wrappings?
Am I afraid to?
Perhaps I've never accepted the gift that I am . . .
Could it be that there is something else inside the wrappings
than what I think there is?
Maybe I've never seen the wonderful gift that I am!
Could the Father's gifts be anything but beautiful?
I love the gifts which those who love me give to me.
Why do I not love this gift of myself from the Father?

And I am a gift to other persons!
Am I willing to be given by the Father to others?
Do others have to be content with the wrappings . . .
never permitted to enjoy the gift?

Every meeting of persons is an exchange of gifts.
But a gift without a giver is not a gift;
it is a thing devoid of a relationship between persons who see themselves
as they truly are: gifts of the Father to each other for others!

A friend is a gift not just to me but to others through me . . .
When I keep my friend—possess him—I destroy his "gift-ness."
If I save his life for me, I lose it;
if I lose it for others, I save it.

Persons are gifts—gifts received and given . . . like the Son!
Friendship is the response of person-gifts to the Father—given.
Friendship is EUCHARIST!

G. Nintemann
(Source Unknown)

Illustration L (for page 43)

Learning Prayer from the Master

Name: _____

Jesus teaches us how to pray. As his disciple, watch how he prays. Go to Jesus and ask him to teach you to pray. The activities in this prayer lab will help you.

Materials

Bible	crayons or markers
pencils	magazines
notebook paper	scissors
large sheets of paper	paste

1. As a group, compose a prayer of a paragraph or two (or a verse or two) asking Jesus to help you to pray.

2. Jesus wants us to pray. Read Matthew 7:7. Write the three verbs in Jesus' command in order:

_____   _____   _____

Circle the first letter of each word above. What do they spell? _____

On a large sheet of paper create a collage that shows what we could pray for. Cut and paste words and pictures from a magazine or draw them.

3. Jesus told two parables that have the same message about prayer:

   The Persistent Friend (Luke 11:5-8)
   The Widow and the Judge (Luke 18:2-8).

Read them and write their message in the banner. Choose characters and act out one of the parables.

4. Match the Bible references with the advice Jesus gives about prayer:

___ Matthew 7:21-23   A. Pray in Jesus' name.
___ Matthew 6:5-6   B. Pray humbly and honestly.
___ Matthew 6:8   C. Keep your prayer short and simple.
___ John 16:23   D. Actions speak louder than words.
___ Luke 18:9-14   E. Pray in private, not to show off.

5. Read some of the following accounts of Jesus at prayer and use them to make a list of five Tips for Praying.

Matthew 11:25   Luke 22:39-42   John 17:1-26   Luke 22:31-32
Luke 4:16   Mark 1:35   Luke 6:12

6. Jesus prayed at important times in his life. Look up the following references and write the occasions when Jesus prayed.

John 11:41-42 _____

Mark 14:36 _____

Luke 3:21-22 _____

Luke 6:12 _____

John 17:6-19 _____

Luke 9:28-29 _____

Luke 23:34, 46 _____

Mark 6:41 _____

Name some significant times when you might pray:

_____

_____

_____

_____

Illustration M (for page 46)

Prayers

Prayer for Peace

Lord, make me an instrument of your
peace;
Where there is hatred, let me sow love;
Where there is injury, pardon;
Where there is doubt, faith;
Where there is despair, hope;
Where there is darkness, light;
And where there is sadness, joy.
O Divine Master, grant that I may not so
much seek
To be consoled as to console;
To be understood as to understand;
To be loved as to love;
For it is in giving that we receive;
It is in pardoning that we are pardoned;
It is in dying that we are born to
Eternal Life.

Learning Christ

Teach me, my Lord, to be sweet and gentle
in all the events of life: in disappointments,
in the thoughtlessness of others, in the in-
sincerity of those I trusted, in the un-
faithfulness of those on whom I relied.

Let me put myself aside, to think of the
happiness of others, to hide my little pains
and heartaches so that I may be the only
one to suffer from them. Teach me to profit
by the suffering that comes across my path.
Let me so use it that it may mellow me, not
harden nor embitter me; that it may make
me patient, not irritable, that it may make
me broad in my forgiveness, not narrow,
haughty or overbearing.

May no one be less good for having
come within my influence. No one less
pure, less true, less kind, less noble for having been a fellow-traveler in our journey
toward Eternal Life.

As I go my rounds from one distraction
to another, let me whisper from time to
time a word of love to you. May my life be
lived in the supernatural, full of power for
good, and strong in its purpose of sanctity.

Radiating Christ

Dear Jesus, help me to spread your fra-
grance everywhere I go: flood my soul
with your spirit and life; penetrate and
possess my whole being so utterly that all
my life may only be a radiance of yours;
shine through me and be so in me that every soul I come in contact with may feel
your presence in my soul. Let them look
up and see no longer me, but only Jesus!
Stay with me and then I shall begin to
shine as you shine, so to shine as a light to
others; the light, O Jesus, will be all from
you; none of it will be mine. It will be you
shining on others through me. Let me thus
praise you in the way which you love
best—by radiating you to those around
me; let me preach you without preaching,
not by my words but by my example, by
the catching force, the sympathetic influence of what I do, the evident fullness of
the love my heart bears to you.

Cardinal John Henry Newman

Prayer of Mary Stuart

Keep me, O Lord, from all pettiness.
Let me be large in thought and word and
deed.

Let me leave off self-seeking and have
done with fault-finding.

Help me to put away all pretense that I
may meet my neighbor face to face, without self-pity and without prejudice.

May I never be hasty in my judgments
but generous to all and in all things.

Make me grow calm, serene, and gentle.

Teach me to put into action my better
impulses and make me straightforward
and unafraid.

Grant that I may realize that it is the tri-
fling things of life that create differences,
that in the higher things we are all one.

And, O Lord God,
Let me not forget to be kind.

Prayer of St. Ignatius

Take, Lord, receive all my liberty, my memory, my understanding, my entire will. Give me only your love and your grace. With these I will be rich enough. I desire nothing more.

Prayer of Cardinal Merry del Val

O dearly beloved Word of God,
teach me to be generous,
to serve you as you deserve,
to give without counting the cost,
to fight without fretting at my wounds,
to labor without seeking rest,
to spend myself without looking for any
    reward
other than that of knowing that
I do your holy will. Amen.

Serenity Prayer

God, grant me the serenity
to accept the things I cannot change,
the courage to change the things I can,
and the wisdom to know the difference.

From the Breastplate of St. Patrick

Christ with me, Christ before me,
Christ behind me;
Christ in me, Christ beneath me,
Christ above me;
Christ on my right, Christ on my left;
Christ in breadth, Christ in length,
Christ in height;
Christ in the heart of every one
    who thinks of me;
Christ in the mouth of every one
    who speaks to me;
Christ in every eye that sees me;
Christ in every ear that hears me.

Memorare

Remember, O most loving Virgin Mary, that never was it known that anyone who fled to your protection, implored your help, or sought your intercession was left unaided. Inspired with this confidence, we turn to you, O virgin of virgins, our Mother. To you we come, before you we stand, sinful and sorrowful. O Mother of the Word Incarnate, do not despise our petitions, but in your mercy hear and answer us. Amen.

Hail, Holy Queen (Salve Regina)

Hail, holy Queen, Mother of Mercy: hail, our life, our sweetness, and our hope! To you do we cry, poor banished children of Eve; to you do we send up our sighs, mourning and weeping in this valley of tears. Turn then, most gracious Advocate, your eyes of mercy toward us; and after this our exile, show us the blessed fruit of your womb, Jesus. O clement, O loving, O sweet Virgin Mary. Amen.

Our Lady of Guadalupe

Our Lady of Guadalupe, mystical rose, intercede for the Church, protect the Holy Father, help all who invoke you in their necessities. Since you are the ever Virgin Mary and Mother of the true God, obtain for us from your most holy Son the grace of a firm faith and a sure hope amid the bitterness of life, as well as an ardent love and the precious gift of final perseverance. Amen.

Spiritual Communion

My Jesus, I believe that you are in the Blessed Sacrament. I love you above all things, and I long for you in my soul. Since I cannot now receive you sacramentally, come at least spiritually into my heart. I embrace you and unite myself entirely to you; never permit me to be separated from you. Amen.

An Act of Contrition

My God, I am sorry for my sins with all my heart. In choosing to do wrong and failing to do good, I have sinned against you whom I should love above all things. I firmly intend, with your help, to do penance, to sin no more, and to avoid whatever leads me to sin. Our Savior Jesus Christ suffered and died for us. In his name, my God, have mercy. Amen.

Illustration N (for page 47)

Letting Go for Love of the Lord

(Have a slip of paper, a pen or pencil, and a small pink or red heart for each participant. Distribute the paper and pens or pencils.)

We are constantly called to conversion, to turn to the Lord, to become better persons. This change in us entails cooperating with the Lord's plan for us. Often it means a letting go, a surrender. In this reflection you will experience how God's love empowers us to give up for his sake what is dear to us.

On the slip of paper write something that is very precious to you that you would find hard to give away or lose. It could be something good like a friend, a special place, or an activity. It could be something harmful that you're attached to, like a fear, a worry, a bad habit, or the dislike of a certain person. . . . Now clench this paper in your fist and close your eyes.

Imagine you are sitting alone in your bedroom, or in chapel, or in your favorite spot. You are reflecting quietly. The door opens and in walks Jesus. He sits down and talks to you a little while. Then he looks down at your hands. "What is that you have?" he asks. "Nothing," you reply, "I can't show you." The two of you talk some more. Then he looks at his hands. He ponders, "What is there I can let go of so that she will let go?"

He thinks of his mother, the most beautiful, wonderful and loving person he knows. "But I can let go of her," he thinks, and his hands begin to open. So he leaves his mother when he begins his public life, when he dies, and again when he ascends into heaven.

He thinks of his friends, those likable men he chose for his constant companions. "That's all right," he decides. "I can let go of them." So Judas betrays him, Peter denies him, and all but one desert him when he needs them most.

He thinks of his good reputation. He was famous, popular. Crowds gathered wherever he was, hailing him as their king. "But I can let go of that too," he thinks. So people turn against him. They mock him, spit upon him, and tell lies about him.

He thinks of his life. How he enjoys sunsets, the boats on the Sea of Galilee, the hills and the green fields, walking in the early morning, breathing the fresh air, laughing with people. "Yes, I can give all that up. I love this person that much," he decides. So, he is scourged, crowned with thorns, crucified, and he dies.

By now his hands are open wide. You can see the scars in them that the nails left. You think, "If he can open his hands for me like that, I can open mine." And you do, slowly. As you open yours, nothing happens at first. Life isn't too different. But little by little it changes; you change. The Lord says to you once more, "May I see that?" You say, "Oh, yes." "May I have it?" he asks. "Oh, certainly," you respond. "May I give you something in return?" Jesus says. And he gives you a priceless gift, the gift of his love flowing into you.
(Assistants take papers from the hands of the participants and replace them with hearts.)
Jesus changes your stony heart into a natural heart to make you more fully human. He fulfills the prophecy of Ezekiel in you:

> I will give them a new heart and put a new spirit within them. I will remove the stony heart from their bodies and replace it with a natural heart (Ezekiel 11:19).

Illustration O (for page 48)

Te Deum

Solo 1:	You are God—
All:	We praise you;
Solo 2:	You are the Lord—
All:	We acclaim you;
Solo 3:	You are the eternal Father:
All:	All creation worships you.

Side 1:	To you all the angels of heaven and all the powers of heaven,
Side 2:	Cherubim and Seraphim, sing in endless praise—
All:	Holy, holy, holy, Lord, God of power and might, heaven and earth are full of your glory.

Boys:	The glorious company of apostles praise you;
Girls:	The noble fellowship of the prophets praise you;
Boys:	The white-robed army of martyrs praise you,
Girls:	Throughout the world Holy Church acclaims you:
All:	Father of majesty unbounded, Your true and only Son, worthy of all worship, And the Holy Spirit, advocate and guide.

Solo 4:	You, O Christ, are the king of glory, the eternal Son of the Father.

Side 1:	When you became man to set us free, you did not spurn the virgin's womb.
Side 2:	You overcame the sting of death and opened the kingdom of heaven to all believers.
Side 1:	You are seated at God's right hand in robes of glory.
Side 2:	We believe that you will come to be our judge.
All:	Come then, Lord, and help your people bought with the price of your own precious blood, and bring us with your saints to glory everlasting.

Illustration P (for page 54)

Loving and Serving as Jesus Did

A station is set up with pitchers of water, basins, and towels. Nearby is a table on which small paper or cloth towels, decorated with hearts, are arranged.

Song

Opening Prayer
God, you are love, and you created us to be like you. Love is shown in deeds. We gather today to think about what this means for us. We ask you to help us love the members of our families, our neighbors, and the people with whom we work and play. Jesus, you taught us how to love. In the gospels we can learn your lessons by listening to your words and studying what you do.

Reading	Matthew 25:31-46 Those who show love will be welcomed into the kingdom on judgment day.
Silent reflection	*Background music is played.*
Reading	John 13:1-15 Jesus washes the feet of the disciples.
Hand washing	*Background music is played.*

Leader: As a sign of our willingness to let God's love flow through us to others we will wash and dry one another's hands, and then take a small towel to remind us to follow Jesus in serving others.

A person goes to the station to pour water. Participants approach the station in pairs. They take turns having water poured over their hands and then having their partner dry them. They take a towel from the table as a memento.

General Intercessions

Response: Lord, hear our prayer.

Side 1:   That we may be willing to go out of our way to help others . . .
Side 2:   That we may be selfless rather than selfish . . .

Side 1:   That we may serve others without expecting anything in return . . .
Side 2:   That we may give generously of our time, talents, and treasures . . .

Side 1:   That our eyes may see things that need to be done . . .
Side 2:   That our ears may hear others' requests . . .

Side 2:   That our hearts may be large enough to serve all people, not only those
            we like . . .

   All: Lord,
            our help and guide,
            make your love the foundation of our lives.
            May our love for you express itself
            in our eagerness to do good for others.
            Grant this through our Lord Jesus Christ, your Son,
            who lives and reigns with you and the Holy Spirit,
            one God, for ever and ever. Amen.

                                    Prayer, 28th Sunday in Ordinary Time

Song

Possible songs:
"Love Is Colored Like a Rainbow," Ray Repp
"God Has Made Us a Family" and "Reach Out," Carey Landry
"They'll Know We Are Christians," Peter Scholtes
"Service," Buddy Caesar
"Sing Out His Goodness," Darryl Ducote
"Whatsoever You Do," Williard F. Jabusch
"Take Christ to the World," Paul Inwood

Illustration Q (for page 62)

The Rosary

Long ago when most people could not read, instead of praying the 150 psalms, they prayed the Hail Mary 150 times. These prayers were in groups of ten called decades, and each decade began with an Our Father. Strings of beads to keep track of the prayers were called "paternosters" (*pater noster* means Our Father). The rosary we pray today has five decades. As we pray a decade, we meditate on an event in the life of Jesus, Mary, and the church called mysteries. There are three sets of mysteries:

Joyful Mysteries: The Annunciation; The Visitation; The Nativity;
The Presentation; The Finding of Jesus in the Temple

Sorrowful Mysteries: The Agony in the Garden; The Scourging;
The Crowning with Thorns; The Carrying of the Cross;
The Crucifixion

Glorious Mysteries: The Resurrection; The Ascension; The Coming of the Holy
Spirit; The Assumption; The Coronation of Mary

We begin the rosary by praying the Apostles Creed on the crucifix and an Our Father, three Hail Marys and a Glory Be on the beads that follow. Then for each decade, we pray an Our Father, ten Hail Marys, and a Glory Be.

In the space below, draw a rosary. Label where the Apostles Creed and Glory Be are prayed. Color the Our Father beads red and the Hail Mary beads blue.

Illustration R (for page 88)

The Lord's Day

"Sunday is the day on which the paschal mystery is celebrated in light of apostolic tradition and is the foremost holy day of obligation in the universal Church."

Code of Canon Law, 1246

"On Sundays and other holy days of obligation the faithful are bound to participate in the Mass; they are also to abstain from those labors and business concerns which impede the worship to be rendered to God, the joy which is proper to the Lord's Day or the proper relaxation of mind and body." Code of Canon Law, 1247

First of the seven duties of Catholic Christians:
"To keep holy the day of the Lord's Resurrection: to worship God by participating in Mass every Sunday and Holy Day of Obligation: to avoid those activities that would hinder renewal of soul and body, e.g., needless work and business activities, unnecessary shopping, etc." National Conference of Catholic Bishops
Basic Teachings for Catholic Religious Education

The LORD said to Moses, "You must also tell the Israelites: Take care to keep my sabbath, for that is to be the token between you and me throughout the generations, to show that it is I, the LORD, who make you holy. Therefore, you must keep the sabbath as something sacred. Whoever desecrates it shall be put to death. If anyone does work on that day, he must be rooted out of his people. Six days there are for doing work, but the seventh day is the sabbath of complete rest, sacred to the LORD. Anyone who does work on the sabbath day shall be put to death. So shall the Israelites observe the sabbath, keeping it throughout their generations as a perpetual covenant. Between me and the Israelites it is to be an everlasting token; for in six days the LORD made the heavens and Earth, but on the seventh day he rested at his ease." Exodus 31:12-17

If you hold back your foot on the sabbath
   from following your own pursuits on my holy day;
If you call the sabbath a delight,
   and the LORD's holy day honorable;
If you honor it by not following your ways,
   seeking your own interests, or speaking with malice—
Then you shall delight in the LORD,
   and I will make you ride on the heights of Earth;
I will nourish you with the heritage of Jacob, your father. Isaiah 58:13-14

"Sunday is the first of all feast days, to be presented to and urged upon the faithful as such, so that it may also become a day of gladness and rest from work."
Constitution on the Sacred Liturgy, 106

"God has a right to demand of man that he dedicate one day of the week to the proper and fitting worship of the eternal Godhead. This should be a day in which the spirit is freed from material preoccupations and enabled to rise up to heavenly concerns. It should be a day when man can examine the secrets of his conscience and thus grasp the binding force of his sacred relations to his Creator.

"The observance of Sunday permits man to promote family unity by making it possible for all the members of the family to enjoy more frequent and harmonious contacts with one another.

"Man has the right to and the need of periodic rest. This permits him to renew the bodily strength used up by hard daily work and likewise to enjoy a decent measure of recreation." *Mater et Magistra*, Pope John XXIII

"The appropriate question to ask ourselves on Sunday evening is: do I approach the beginning of a new week with more serenity, tranquility, joy and faith than I was conscious of last Friday evening? If we have not had experiences throughout the weekend that deepened our faith, that heightened our religious sensitivity, that bring a bit more of tranquility and serenity into our lives, then religiously speaking, the weekend has been a waste." *The Sinai Myth*, Andrew Greeley

"Those who walked in ancient customs came to a new hope, no longer sabbatizing, but living the Lord's day, on which we came to live through him and his death."
Ignatius of Antioch

"The sabbaths are our great cathedrals."
Rabbi Abraham Heschel

Illustration S (for page 100)

Written Meditation on Luke 8:40-48

Retelling of the story

I was in the crowd of people hurrying after Jesus, noisy and jostling one another in the hot sun. We were curious to see him heal Jairus's daughter. At times Jesus was so enveloped by people, I lost sight of him. Suddenly, the mob came to a standstill. Over the shoulder of the man in front of me I could see Jesus facing the crowd and searching for someone. I heard him say, "Who touched my clothing?" One of his disciples said, "You can see how this crowd hems you in, yet you ask, 'Who touched me?'" Jesus continued to look about. Then a woman came forth trembling. She fell at his feet in fear, and we could hear her voice, breathless and shaking, as she told her story. Jesus put his hand on her head and raised her up gently. He looked into her face and said, "Daughter, it is your faith that has cured you. Go in peace and be free of this illness."

Being alone with Jesus

That night, walking by the lake with Jesus, I brought up the incident.

Conversation with Jesus

"Too bad that woman had to wait so long to be cured." "Yes," said Jesus. "If she had joined the others in the crowds to be cured, she could have been helped earlier. And the way she tried to do it—secretly—almost as if she feared I would have refused her."

"I'm like that, too, sometimes," I commented. "I run around, troubled and complaining, trying certain remedies to make myself feel better and ignore your aid. It's as if I don't apply what I say I believe. You do have power to help me. You do want to help me. You are interested in my life. Most of all, you do love me—unconditionally, as Father said last night."

"You're right," Jesus said. "I'm always ready to help you, to pick you up when you fall, to heal your wounds and hug away your hurts. Why don't you come to me?"

"Because you're invisible. I can't really see you or feel your presence."

"But that doesn't mean I'm not real. Let yourself be open to the power of my love in your life, and you'll see just how real I am."

"OK. What about the sicknesses I came to see in myself during this retreat? Can you take away those pains?"

"What do you think? Don't you remember how afraid you were each time you had to drive? You thought you'd never overcome your fear. Then all of a sudden it disappeared. You're not a hopeless case. But remember, even if you are fearful and imperfect, no matter how many capital sins you have, I still love you. Trust me. Haven't I always taken care of you up to now?"

"Yes, Lord."

Prayer Checkup

You shall love the Lord your God
with all your heart,
with all your being,
with all your strength,
and with all your mind.
Luke 10:27

In the morning

Do I . . .
say good morning to the Lord?
thank and praise God for another
     day?
pray the Morning Offering?
ask God's help in making
     decisions?
pray for the grace to do the right
     things and avoid sin?

During the day

Do I . . .
think of God?
pray grace before and after meals?
turn to God in times of trouble?
ask God's help?
see God in others?
pray during free moments?
thank and praise God when I see
one of God's gifts?

2

In the evening

Do I . . .
think over the events of the day?
ask God to bless my family,
relatives, and friends?
pray for people who need help?
thank God for the good things
that happened during the day?
express sorrow for my failures
to love?
ask God to help me to be a better
Christian tomorrow?

3

During the month

Do I . . .
pray with the church?
participate at Mass?
join in special parish prayer times?
read the Bible?
pray the rosary?
pray the stations of the cross?

Do I . . .
take time for personal prayer?
spend extra time with the Lord?
pray prayers such as the Hail Mary,
     the Our Father, and the Glory Be?
pray my favorite prayers such as
     the Peace Prayer of St. Francis?

4

Other Titles by Sister Mary Kathleen Glavich:

Acting Out the Miracles and Parables

52 playlets for grades 1-12 that will enliven and enrich religion classes.
ISBN: 0-89622-363-9, 142 pp, $12.95

Leading Students Into Scripture

Presents a wide range of methods to help children understand the Bible.
ISBN: 0-89622-328-0, 112 pp, $9.95

Gospel Plays for Students
36 Scripts for Education & Worship

Favorite and less familiar Gospel events scripted in easy-to-understand language for children of all ages.
ISBN: 0-89622-407-4, 112 pp, $12.95

Available at religious bookstores or from

TWENTY-THIRD PUBLICATIONS
P.O. Box 180 • Mystic, CT 06355
1-800-321-0411